D1636918

Savannah Style

Savannah Style

Mystery and Manners

By Susan Sully

Photographs by Steven Brooke

Foreword by John Berendt

RIZZOLI
NEW YORK

First published in the United States of America in 2001 by
Rizzoli International Publications, Inc.
300 Park Avenue South
New York, NY 10010

ISBN: 0-8478-2376-8
LC: 00-111212

Front cover: Interior, The Francis Sorrel House.

Page 2: Interior, Home of Francis McNairy. Built 1860.

*Pages 4–5: This cast iron fountain, designed by Janes, Beebe and Company of
New York in 1858, creates a dramatic focal point in Forsyth Park, the European
style garden that forms the southern border of Oglethorpe's system of wards.*

Page 8: Mint juleps being served at Lebanon Plantation.

Distributed by St. Martin's Press

Printed and bound in Singapore

To Celia Dunn,
who holds the key to so many doors and
hearts in Savannah, and

to John Duncan,
whose great knowledge of Savannah's
architecture is rivaled only by his
admiration for it.

For the indescribable charm about its
streets and buildings, its parks and squares
. . . there is but one Savannah. Without a
rival, without an equal, it stands unique.
—Timothy Harley, 1885

Wherever men have lived and moved and had their
being, hoped, feared, succeeded, failed, loved, laughed,
been happy, lost, mourned, died, were beloved or
detested, there remains forever after a something,
intangible and tenuous as thought, a sentience very like
a soul, which abides forever in the speechless walls.
—John Bennett, *The Doctor to the Dead*, 1946

Contents

Foreword

by John Berendt

The first time I set foot in Savannah, it was my great good fortune to be shown around town by a sixth-generation grande dame who knew every leaf and stone and did not mince words. She took me on a tour of the lush, garden-like squares and walked me through several house museums. As we moved around the city, she made a point of showing me the buildings, gardens, ironwork, statuary, trees, and even a vine or two that were her favorites, the things she liked most about Savannah. Then she told me what she liked least about Savannah.

"Outsiders!" she said, looking me square in the eye. "The ones who fall in love with Savannah on a visit, move here, and then tell us how much more lively and prosperous Savannah could be if we only knew what we had and how to take advantage of it. We smile pleasantly and we nod, but we don't budge an inch." The woman paused for emphasis and then went on, slowly and deliberately, as if reciting a mantra, "We happen . . . to like things . . . just . . . the way . . . they are!"

I subsequently lived in Savannah for five years, and what I learned in that time was that if the city has a single guiding principle, those ten words would be it. They reflect a sentiment that goes far deeper than a mere resistance to change. Savannah has a reverence for the past and for a way of life that has been three centuries in the making. Savannah's collective memory has been seasoned by two major wars, three cycles of financial boom and bust, two disastrous fires, and five deadly epidemics. They are all part of the mix. What William Faulkner once said about the South in general is especially true of Savannah: "The past is not dead. It isn't even past."

Savannah's past is present in every aspect of its ambience (the squares, for example). One of Georgia's original missions was to serve as a military buffer between the Spanish in Florida and the English colonies to the

north, so when James Oglethorpe laid out Savannah in 1733 he used the configuration of a Roman military encampment as one of his design sources. He grouped dwellings and public buildings around four open spaces in which amenities such as water pumps, markets, and baking ovens would be placed, and into which people and livestock could be gathered in case of an enemy attack. Oglethorpe's street layout became a template for Savannah's eventual expansion, and his bare and dusty squares evolved over time into the embowered Edens they are today.

During my stay in Savannah, I noticed a pronounced Anglophilia. I saw it in the architecture (especially the period Regency buildings, which are extremely rare elsewhere in America) and in Savannah's preference for English furniture. This tilt toward things English sometimes takes odd forms. The Queen's birthday, for example, is frequently celebrated by the Savannah branch of the English Speaking Union, at the Andrew Low House, which is headquarters of the Georgia chapter branch of the Colonial Dames. There is a reason for all this. By 1733, when Georgia was established as the last of the thirteen colonies by George II, English shipping dominated the Atlantic coast, eclipsing the influence of France, Spain, and the Netherlands, all of which had enjoyed close ties to the older colonies and had left their imprint on each of them. So Georgia became the most thoroughly English of all the colonies.

I haven't quite figured out whether the English are responsible for Savannah's manners, but they are exemplary in any case and apparently always have been. James Buckingham, an Englishman who toured America in 1839, wrote that Savannahians are "characterized by great elegance in all their deportment; the men are perfect gentlemen in their manners, and the women are accomplished ladies." Compared with northern women, he said, the women of Savannah "were in general dressed in better taste, less showily and less expensively, but with more simple elegance in form, and more chasteness in colour." That squares with my own private assessment of Savannah. I judge manners by timing how long it takes a person to say goodbye: the longer the goodbye, the more gracious and mannerly the person. We northerners can be rather abrupt at leave taking; Savannahians linger twenty minutes on average while saying goodbye. They have better manners.

Given all this refinement, it is probably not surprising that one of the greatest social arbiters in American history was a Savannahian, Ward MacAllister. It was MacAllister who in 1892 conceived the concept of "the first 400," a list, drawn up by MacAllister himself, of the cream of New York society. MacAllister regularly passed judgment on the worthiness of socialites, composing list after list, one of which was entitled "Ten Ladies Who could Gracefully Cross a Ballroom Floor Unescorted."

In periods of prosperity, Savannah achieved dazzling heights of wealth and importance. In the year 1819, for example, President James Monroe came to Savannah to witness the departure of the S.S. Savannah for England— the first steamship to make a transatlantic crossing. This event was the equivalent, then, of the first manned flight to the moon. It put Savannah at the center of the most exciting events of the day. At the outbreak of the Civil War in 1861, Savannah was one of the world's biggest cotton-shipping ports, and one of the richest cities in America.

Clearly, the financial crashes that occurred in 1820 and then again after the Civil War were demoralizing to Savannah. Savannah withdrew in isolation behind its moat of piney woods and marshland, clinging proudly to the remnants of its glorious past. For most of the twentieth century, Savannah was impoverished, but nonetheless its civic leaders fought off developers who wanted to cut roads through the squares and pave them over as parking lots, and they successfully battled those who had begun the wholesale demolition of Savannah's historic houses to make way for gas stations and the like.

It isn't just the squares and the houses that Savannahians value so highly. It's the scale of the city and its leisurely pace of life. They've preserved it very well, in my opinion. Recently, I asked a Savannah gentleman to explain Savannah to me in as few words as possible. "This is a city," he said, "where men own their own white tie and tails. We don't rent them." Figure that any way you wish. As far as I'm concerned, it says it all.

Lace curtain detail, The Francis Sorrel House.

Introduction: Mystery and Manners

by Susan Sully

A bronze statue of James Oglethorpe by Daniel Chester French dominates Chippewa Square.

Savannah is a place defined by paradox. An old worldly city financed by new world fortunes, it is populated by citizens who are renowned for both their exquisite manners and their mysterious eccentricities. Founded by philanthropists, made to flourish by capitalists, rescued from destruction by a combination of benign neglect and ardent preservation, it has endured through centuries of mercurial fortune. Since its establishment in 1733, Savannah has existed in a state of perpetual tension between opposing forces: generosity and greed, ambition and despair, progress and disaster, growth and decay, decadence and decorum. All of these forces have left their mark upon the city's streets, walls, gardens, and rooms. It is this residue of history that makes the city so captivating and alluring, drawing visitors and residents alike deep into communion with it as they alternately seek to understand it and simply surrender to the complexities that express Savannah's enigmatic soul.

To those who first encounter Savannah as tourists or new residents, these contradictions are immediately evident in the physical surroundings. A garden city, Savannah is at once undeniably urban, with busy traffic and densely built blocks, and surprisingly bucolic, with avenues of trees, verdant squares, and private courtyards that overgrow their bounds in spring with dangling vines of Lady Banksia roses. "Savannah looks as if 30,000 people had gone out from town into a bowery forest glade, and, without disturbing its silence or its beauty, made summer-houses amidst its flowers and plants and under the shade of its spreading trees," wrote one enthralled visitor in 1871.[1] Although omnibuses and eighteen wheelers now frequent the city's streets, residents and visitors still find time to rest within its squares or linger on its sidewalks, cool beneath the shade of overarching trees. When New York author John Berendt came to visit in the 1980s, and then decided to remain for eight years while writing his bestseller, *Midnight in the*

Garden of Good and Evil, he remarked that strolling through its squares was like "walking through the rooms of a magnificent open-air mansion."[2]

The source of this balance between natural beauty and structured civilization can be traced back to the plan founding father James Oglethorpe brought with him when he arrived in Savannah in 1733 along with 114 settlers. While scholars vary widely in their thoughts regarding the origins of this plan, arguing that its inspiration may have come from places as far-flung as ancient Rome, Georgian London, and Peking, they all agree that it is outstanding in its efficiency and endurance as well as its elegance. "I went myself to view the Savannah River," wrote Oglethorpe in a letter soon after he arrived. "I fixed upon a healthy situation about ten miles from the sea. The river here forms a half moon, along the south side of which the banks are almost forty foot high and on top flat, which they call a bluff. Ships that draw twelve foot water can ride within ten yards of the bank. Upon the river side in the center of this plain, I have laid out the town."

A view of Savannah drawn by Peter Gordon in 1734 shows a small area bordered on three sides by woods and one by water where intersecting streets are evenly spaced around four open squares. These were the first four wards laid out by Oglethorpe. While his intention in creating the open squares was largely utilitarian, "for a market place and for exercising the Inhabitants," their ultimate value was to prove largely ornamental. "Originally naked, open muddy spaces, abandoned to wallowing swine, the squares were landscaped and ornamented with sculpture and fountains in the nineteenth century," explains preservationist and architectural historian Mills B. Lane in his book *Savannah Revisited: History and Architecture*. Describing the early stages of these improvements in 1810, Robert Mackay wrote, "The alterations in the squares [are] so great an improvement that Savannah is quite fascinating. Every square in town is now enclosed with light cedar posts painted white and a chain along their tops, trees planted within and two paved footpaths across, the remainder of the ground they are spreading bermuda grass over, and upon the whole [the] town looks very enchanting."[3]

So livable was Oglethorpe's plan that twenty more such wards were created over a period of 120 years. With no more city-owned space remaining for such orderly growth, planners and developers finally abandoned the plan in the southern regions of the city, even though they still invoked its principles when designing the automobile suburbs of Ardsley Park and Chatham Crescent in the early twentieth century. As each new square and ward was designated, it was named in honor of one of Savannah's reigning heroes and this nomenclature reveals the shifting values that shaped the city's destiny.

Honorees include Oglethorpe, who established Savannah not as a royal colony but as a benevolent trusteeship to provide a haven for prison inmates and persecuted foreign protestants, and John Reynolds, the first royal governor of Georgia, who transformed the colony from a failed philanthropic venture into a productive member of England's imperialist economy. They include war heroes who defended Savannah against Spanish attack in the early 18th century and English attack during the American Revolution, engaged in naval conflicts with England during the War of 1812, and battled the Federal Army during the Civil War. Monuments erected in the squares during the nineteenth century pay homage to an even more diverse group of men including a king, a minister, and several merchant princes. Contrary to logic, the statues commemorating famous men were rarely installed in their correspondingly named squares. In what Lane calls "a spontaneous but eccentric development,

Savannah now has monuments to Nathanael Greene in Johnson Square but not in Greene Square, to Pulaski in Monterey Square but not in Pulaski Square, to Oglethorpe in Chippewa Square but not in Oglethorpe Square."[4] To make matters even more complicated, many of the wards that encompass each square fail to share the same name. Wright Square is in Percival Ward, Telfair Square is in Heathcote Ward, and Madison Square, in Jasper Ward.

However much these inconsistencies may baffle visitors, they are entirely consistent with Savannah's character. While its history can be written in sentences that run from left to right on neatly numbered pages describing events in sequential order, that is not how Savannah reveals its past. In this small city where so much has happened in so little time—fortunes made and lost, rulers celebrated and deposed, and styles embraced and discarded over a period of little more than 250 years—history is omnipresent. Impulses, ideals, and events are inscribed upon the city in simultaneously visible layers like the shadowy writing on a palimpsest.

Consider, for example, the fact that Savannah's landmark district is an area composed almost entirely of nineteenth century buildings arrayed within an eighteenth century plan. Note also that, while many of these buildings remain faithful to the tastes of a specific period, others display, on single facades, the hallmarks of a range of architectural styles spanning decades and even centuries of changing tastes. To discover the solution to these aesthetic puzzles, one must delve into the annals of the city's tragedies and victories, emerging at last with a sense of wonder that these buildings have survived at all.

A Mercurial History

When Savannah was just a struggling settlement populated largely by what one historian described as "a parcel of poor people . . . incapable of living at home," bricks were too expensive and labor intensive to prove a popular building material. Instead, the majority of Savannah's 18th-century homes were constructed from the plentiful native timber. "In the past two or three years much building has been going on in the city," wrote a visitor in 1762. "At present there are about 200 houses. Of these I have seen but three of brick."[5] Although the city began to flourish in the second half of the eighteenth century under the supervision of three royal governors, its structures were still composed largely of wood. In 1796, a fire sparked in a bakehouse and quickly spread. Over the next six hours, the conflagration raged throughout the city, destroying more than half its buildings—an estimated 229 houses and 146 outbuildings.

Just three years before this disastrous incident razed whole neighborhoods, a quiet event occurred just beyond the city limits that was to catalyze a whole century of economic growth. In 1793, an enterprising Yale graduate named Eli Whitney invented the cotton gin on a plantation outside of Savannah. He described his invention as "a machine with which one man will clean ten times as much cotton as he can in any other way before known and also cleanse it much better than with the usual mode."[6] This innovation, combined with the increasing cultivation of cotton throughout the Georgia colony from the sea islands to the Piedmont region, ushered in the era of the Cotton Kingdom, of which Savannah was one of four leading ports. Huge fortunes began to be amassed as Savannahians solidified their trade patterns with England and Northern cities. "By 1818, the place had become the sixteenth largest city in America, with exports of more than $14,000,000. By then the city's trade was considerable, with thirteen regular ships to England, fifteen packet brigs and schooners to New York, two or three to Philadelphia, Baltimore and Boston, two or three sloops to Charleston, and four or five vessels to the West Indies,"[7] wrote Lane in his study of the city.

While Savannahians exported cotton and other products, they imported luxuries of all kind—fine fabrics, crystal and china, furniture, and delicacies to eat and drink— and attracted craftsmen capable of building new homes and civic structures, which reflected the city's growing status as a new world center of commerce. Due to the monolithic nature of this cotton-based economy and the constantly shifting political and economic patterns of America as a developing nation, the foundation upon which this new prosperity was built was far from stable. Throughout the reign of the Cotton Kingdom, the city was vulnerable to spectacular booms and busts, which fueled periodic cycles of building and decay. When nineteenth century Savannahians had money, they spend it boldly, beautifully, and conspicuously. When hard times fell, the city quickly attained an air of gloom and decrepitude. This mercurial environment fostered a carpe diem approach to architecture and decoration: live gorgeously today, for tomorrow you may go broke.

Descriptions of Savannah recorded in letters, diaries, and published accounts during the last three centuries provide a vivid appreciation of the ebb and flow of fortune that shaped Savannah's history. In 1791, traveling diarist John Pope declared somewhat prematurely, "Savannah is, and ever will be, a Place of Opulence, so long as human Nature shall require Food and Raiment or Commerce spread her Canvas to the Wind."[8] While the conclusion of the War of 1812 ushered in a new era of prosperity for the city, as trade flowed more freely with English and other American ports, the city's physical appearance still fell short of the standards of visitors from more established urban areas. In 1815, Herman Stebbins of New York wrote, "Savannah appeared like a poor city in ruins. There is not half a dozen good buildings in the whole city and not one elegant one."

This sweeping denunciation failed to acknowledge the early stirrings of Savannah's architectural excellence, as demonstrated in the handsome homes being designed by northern craftsmen including John Ash, Isaiah Davenport, and Amos Scudder, who worked in the Georgian and Federal styles. In 1817, Savannah welcomed its first professionally trained English architect, the young William Jay. During his brief tenure in Savannah, Jay designed almost a dozen buildings that expressed the elegant neoclassicism popular in Regency England, becoming one of the city's most celebrated architects. But his heyday was short-lived, curtailed by a series of misfortunes that shattered his hopes for new world fame and fortune.

"In 1820 there was another disastrous fire, in which 463 houses were destroyed" wrote Charles Hardee in *Reminiscences and Recollections of Old Savannah*.[9] "In this same year Savannah was visited by a severe equinoctial storm and an epidemic of yellow fever. Pretty hard luck for a struggling little city of seven thousand to have three such calamities on one year! Don't you think so?" And if these disasters were not trouble enough, 1820 also marked the onset of a national depression which crippled Savannah's economy for nearly a decade. Fleeing back to England from the desperate city, Jay described it as "A Niobe of cities, a chaos of Ruins… rising a model, fallen a monument."[10] More than a decade later, Irish comedian Tyrone Power visited Savannah and remarked in his journal that it had a "decayed look, which is so melancholy and which nowhere arrives sooner than in this climate."[11] But another visitor touring the town in the same year formed a much more

Loading cotton at the port of Savannah, circa 1903–07
(Photograph from the collection of the Library of Congress, courtesy of Historic Savannah Foundation)

sanguine impression. "These manifold grassy parks . . . are very picturesque and inviting, and highly suggestive of health and comfort," Sara Hathaway exclaimed. "They are alive and musical with the glee of groups of happy children.... One would think life was all sunshine."

"Savannah is the most charming of cities, and reminds me of 'the maiden in the green-wood[,]'" Swedish novelist Fredrika Bremer declared in her 1854 volume, *Homes of the New World*.[12] "It is . . . an assemblage of villas which have come together for company. In each quarter is a green marketplace, surrounded with magnificent, lofty trees; and in the centre of each verdant market-place leaps up a living fountain, a spring of fresh water, gushing forth, shining in the sun, and keeping the green-sward moist and cool. Savannah might be called the city of the gushing springs; there can not be, in the whole world, a more beautiful city than Savannah." A year later, visiting English novelist, William Thackeray wrote a letter that opens, " . . . I write from the most comfortable quarters I have ever had in the United States . . . the house of my friend Andrew Low of the great house of A. Low and Co., Cotton Dealers, brokers, Merchants—what's the word?...They are tremendous men these cotton merchants."[13]

By the time these last two accounts were penned, Savannah had attained a peak of prosperity supported by the ever-expanding cotton trade and within this promising environment, a new generation of architects were plying their trade. The best of these included Irish-born Charles Cluskey, who designed a number of homes in the Greek Revival style and a host of robust commercial buildings located along the riverfront area that was named Factors Row in honor of the cotton factors who worked there. Another leading architect of the time, John Norris, came from New York to complete prominent commissions included the Greek Revival Custom House and Andrew Low House, the Gothic Revival Green-Meldrim House, and the Italianate Mercer House.

Since fires had consumed nearly all of the 18th-century frame houses that once lined the downtown wards, new houses were constructed over their ruins, creating a brick and masonry city where once a modest wooden village sat. Successions of town houses were constructed in the middle of the blocks, with many homes attached as double- or row-houses. Large single dwelling houses were often placed on either ends of the blocks and on the trust lots, areas the size

of full city blocks that were originally reserved in Oglethorpe's plan for public and commercial structures. In the nineteenth century, these became the sites for magnificent mansions commissioned by the city's merchant princes. Despite the increasing variety of architectural styles employed, the houses maintained a certain consistency through both the raised basements employed to elevate the entrances above the sandy, dirty streets and the prevalence of decorative iron stair railings and balconies.

Wealth continued to mount in Savannah until the mid-19th century when the city was suddenly isolated and commerce was throttled by the onset of the Civil War. Cut off from the sea in 1862 by the fall of Fort Pulaski near the mouth of the Savannah River, Savannah was plunged into a quiet state of dread and anticipation that was to last until the city surrendered with little resistance to General Sherman in 1864. A visitor to Savannah during the Federal blockade described the eerie mood that prevailed for two full years. "A strange, mysterious weird quietude reigns perpetually. Stagnation and paralysis obstruct the channels where business briskly flowed. The whole town—everything—seems to have halted in the precise attitude of one who, with respiration suspended, is listening all agape for some undefined announcement to be made."

That announcement came near the conclusion of the war, when invading General Sherman telegraphed President Abraham Lincoln with these words: "I beg to present you, as a Christmas gift, the city of Savannah, with one hundred and fifty guns and plenty of ammunition, also about twenty-five thousand bales of cotton." One of the most infamous quotations concerning Savannah's history, these few words offer clues that help to explain why Savannah survived with nearly all its antebellum architecture intact when so many other Southern cities fell to Sherman's wrath. While Sherman was largely influenced in his decision not to destroy the city by the fact that its citizens, including cotton merchants who were eager to resume their trade, surrendered without resistance, he may also have been swayed by the sheer beauty of the place. Certainly, Savannahians made sure that the Federal troops were housed comfortably during their occupation of the city, with one of its most prominent English-born cotton merchants, Charles Green, offering Sherman the use of his mansion for several months.

While the nearby port of Charleston languished under the post-war Reconstruction government, Savannah regained vitality relatively quickly as its port resumed commerce with Northern cities within months of the war's end. Savannah reached new heights of financial vitality in the late nineteenth century, exporting up to two million bales of cotton annually. As proponents of the New South economy grew rich, they remodeled older buildings and commissioned new houses and public buildings in the flamboyant styles popular at the time. Savannah's already eclectic architecture grew even more varied as Federal and Greek Revival facades and interiors received new ornamentation in the highly decorative Second Empire baroque and Renaissance Revival styles. Italianate homes begun before the war were lavishly completed and furnished with opulent interior detail. New homes in the fanciful Queen Anne and Romanesque Revival styles were built as the city expanded toward the south. Architects from Paris, New York, and Boston vied for commissions financed by the once more vibrant cotton trade.

Beaux-Arts trained Detlef Lienau, a founder of the American Institute of Architects, introduced the Second Empire Baroque style to the city, "applying vivacious relief surfaces to the older staid Greek Revival buildings."[14] Harvard graduate William Gibbons Preston, working in a style closely related to the Romanesque Revival mode popularized by Henry Hobson Richardson, received multiple commissions including the new Cotton Exchange, the grand DeSoto Hotel, and a mansion for entrepreneur George Baldwin. Working in a similar vein, Alfred Eichberg designed a host of brick villas featuring semiround turrets with conical roofs, fanciful chimneys, and molded terra cotta details.

Modern Day Destruction, Decay, and Preservation

While new buildings were constructed, old ones began to be torn down to make room for progress. Although their city had escaped the destruction of Sherman's brutal March to the Sea, Savannahians themselves often showed less respect for their august architecture as the demands of modern living and shifting tastes influenced new generations of inhabitants. As the devastating effects of the boll weevil on Georgia's cotton crops began to slow the business of the port in the early decades of the 20th century, and the introduction of street car and automobile transportation led to the popularity of new suburbs, Savannah's older wards began to fall into a state of urban decay that gradually deepened over several decades.

The port of Savannah, circa 1949–50
(Photograph from the Ellis collection, circa 1949–50, courtesy of Historic Savannah Foundation)

"[T]he beholder will have pleasure enough in the many lovely old mansions in the heart of the city, or where the heart once was before its life went to find other residence in the ever-enlarging suburbs," wrote W.D. Howells in an article describing Savannah for *Harper's Magazine* in 1919. "These very characteristic and memorable mansions can still be counted by scores, but every now and then one of them disappears through natural causes, as well as through that effect of bad taste which asserts itself everywhere, or from some real or imaginary public demand."[15] A single, short, shocking quotation from Lady Astor, in which she described Savannah as "a lovely woman with a dirty face," suffices to describe the decrepit and abandoned air that characterized the city at its nadir of urban decay in the middle decades of the twentieth century.

By then, a massive exodus to the suburbs had sucked much of the residential population from downtown Savannah. While the city still served as a vital hub for the several railroad lines that terminated there, transporting a variety of raw and manufactured goods to and from Savannah's port, the grand homes that had once housed the mercantile elite fell into disrepair. While many of these were abandoned or demolished, valued more for the price of their bricks than their beautiful appearance, others were carelessly subdivided into tenements to house the workers who kept the city's economy afloat. Railroad employees requiring a place to rest between trips slept in ornate rooms furnished with plain bunk beds and lit by naked light bulbs. Soldiers stationed in the city during the Second World War crowded in amidst the opulent chambers that once accommodated Savannah's most elegant entertainments. Members of the professional classes who lived in Ardsley Park and Chatham Crescent remodeled formal parlors and dining rooms to serve as downtown offices. The squares that once provided gracious outdoor living rooms for all of Savannah's citizens languished under neglect, becoming overgrown and even dangerous. The warehouses, offices, and temples to commerce that crowded the riverfront fell into decay as the once bustling port assumed a seedy air. The formerly vibrant city attained a moribund quality that ranged in mood from deeply sad to downright sinister.

City leaders and business people seeking to restore vitality to the fading area began to launch often misguided efforts to reshape the town to meet the needs of modern commerce. "[M]erchants began knocking down old

During the mid-20th century, abandoned houses and unkempt shrubbery bordered the sidewalks of downtown Savannah. (Photograph courtesy of Historic Savannah Foundation)

buildings to make way for gas stations, parking lots, and commercial structures. They also drew a bead on the squares, proposing to pave them over as parking lots or at least slice roadways through the middle of them," wrote Berendt in his foreword to the *National Trust Guide to Savannah*.[16] Unwilling to stand by and watch the destruction of the city that had so elegantly accommodated two centuries of Savannahians, a small group of concerned citizens began mobilizing in a preservation movement. Starting in the 1930s, this movement gained momentum in 1955 when the city's public market was demolished to public dismay. That same year, a group of ladies who were veterans of that fight rescued the Isaiah Davenport House—one of Savannah's finest Federal mansions—from the wrecking ball. These seven ladies went on to found Historic Savannah Foundation, which ultimately succeeded in rescuing and restoring more than 1100 architecturally significant buildings. Crucial funding for this massive restoration movement was provided through the creation of a revolving fund for the purchase of endangered properties, initiated in 1960 by a group of preservation-minded businessmen.

Working independently or in groups including the Society for the Preservation of the Squares of Savannah and the Savannah Landmark Rehabilitation Project, Savannahians and interested outsiders began to reclaim the city's former glory. Historic Savannah Foundation used the tactic of hospitality to lure visitors into restored downtown homes, hosting the annual Savannah Tour of Homes, which raised both money and the heightened awareness needed to fuel ongoing preservation efforts. By setting up the revolving fund and encouraging new residents to acquire and restore threatened houses, the Foundation catalyzed a repopulation movement that today is spreading throughout the downtown area. City efforts, including the redesign of the old riverfront into a visitor-friendly zone, refashioned Savannah as a mecca for tourists seeking history and architectural beauty. And the restoration and creative reuse of more than 35 major buildings ranging from an 1892 armory, a 1925 department store and a 1946 theater by the Savannah College of Art and Design have created unusual educational facilities for a growing student body that is injecting a new level of energy to the once abandoned streets and squares.

One of the most notable and ultimately notorious members of Savannah's preservation movement was Jim

The Isaiah Davenport House, one of the city's finest Federal mansions, was converted into tenements during the 1930s. (Photograph courtesy of Historic Savannah Foundation)

Williams, the antiques dealer whose life and death were so colorfully chronicled by Berendt in *Midnight in the Garden of Good and Evil*. Having come into a fortune through a phenomenally profitable real estate venture, Williams turned his proceeds toward preservation, purchasing, and restoring "almost a score of notable houses and up to forty buildings essential to the historic scene across the city."[17] Ranging from modest cottages to massive mansions, these houses reflected the full range of Savannah's architectural tastes and styles. It was in one of these, an opulent Italianate structure called Mercer House, that the most dramatic event in Williams's extraordinary life was to occur—the shooting death of his part-time employee Danny Hansford—for which Williams was tried an unprecedented four times and ultimately acquitted.

"There have actually been *three* violent deaths in this house," Williams informed Berendt during an interview.[18] While the other two deaths were unquestionably accidental—one young man fell from the roof and another tumbled down the stairs—an air of mystery inevitably clings to a place where so many lives have ended tragically. And yet, this sense of mystery is nearly obscured by the multi-layered veil of manners that envelopes the house. The serenely symmetrical facade is relatively restrained, considering the Victorian excesses that were to find architectural expression in the decades that followed its 1860s construction. Set well back from the street behind an iron fence, the house seems more to enclose itself rather than to gesture boldly across the square it faces. But this polite composure conceals, rather than reveals, the extravagant interior which Williams, in Berendt's words, transformed "into something greater than its former grandeur. He replaced several plain Victorian mantels with more elaborately carved mantels of classical design, he hung crystal chandeliers and he converted three adjoining rooms on the second floor into one grand room—a ballroom, complete with a functioning pipe organ."[19]

While respecting the more refined aspects of the city's aesthetic traditions in his restoration of the exterior, Williams reveled in the grand manner of the suddenly rich 19th century Savannahians when decorating the interior rooms of his mansion. Due to the sensational popularity of Berendt's book and the movie, based on it, Mercer House has become one of the most visited sites in all of Savannah. A stream of tourists stop before its fence to gaze upon the scene of the now famous killing and to take pictures in front of it. But the house's enduring appeal may also stem from its peculiar ambiance as a meeting ground for mystery and manners —two defining attributes of Savannah itself.

While the mysteries that surround Mercer House are writ large, little mysteries abound throughout the homes and gardens in Savannah. Some of these are simple riddles posed by strange juxtapositions of anachronistic elements. Why, for example, is an early-19th-century mantelpiece from a downtown mansion designed by William Jay now situated in a Mediterranean Revival villa in Ardsley Park? Why were the elaborate faux-bois walls of the dining room in the Champion, Harper-Fowlkes House hidden for decades behind panels of patterned wallpaper? Why did one great house by William Jay, the Owens-Thomas House, survive virtually unchanged through two centuries of natural and man-made destruction when so many others were destroyed or obscured by extensive remodelings? These are simple questions of "who dunnit" and "why" that can be answered by studying the history of Savannah and its people. But there are also deeper, more impenetrable mysteries that pervade the city and permeate its streets and rooms and gardens.

There is the strangely sinister mood that cloaks the back ways of Factors Row. While the tourist attractions lining the river's edge lend a carnival atmosphere to the once commercial spot, the stone and brick passageways that wind behind the buildings and underneath their pedestrian bridges are as silent and dank as tombs. Conversely, Savannah's cemeteries, final resting grounds for those who perished in fires, epidemics, and wars, have an almost cheerful, park-like feel. They are popular destinations for residents and tourists alike, who wander their tree-lined paths and consume picnics and even cocktails by the graves.

There is the surprising insouciance with which Savannahians accommodate souvenirs of death and violence in rooms devoted to mirth and hospitality. A gory image of Judith displaying the decapitated head of Holfernes dominates one wall in a guest room decorated with heavy velvet draperies that reflect the Italian painting's carmine hues. Taxidermied birds and skeletal remains of fish and other animals populate the corners of a room tucked beneath the slanted eaves of a fine Federal house. A Dickensian depiction of an emaciated miser glares down from his frame at a dining table bedecked with brightly shining silver, crystal, and porcelain. This same painting hung in Jim Williams's study the night of the fatal shooting.

Finally, there is Savannahians' curious nostalgia not just for the glory days of their city, but also for the genteel decay that characterized its slow decline. While some Savannahians choose to restore their homes to shining splendor as perfect reproductions of antebellum elegance, others prefer to celebrate the tarnished beauty of the Cotton Kingdom in decline. One couple cleaned antique gilt cornices just enough to reveal the gleam of gold but not so much as to render them perfectly shining. When a chunk of plaster cloth fell from one man's bedroom ceiling, nearly crushing him beneath its weight, he removed the remaining plaster cloth and left the ceiling's aged and cracking plaster bare, coating it with varnish to enhance its yellowed tone. Another Savannahian purposefully collects antiques, which, though fine, proudly reveal their signs of age and use with chips, dents, and *craquelure*.

These peculiarities point to the larger tragedy of Savannah and the South, a region that experienced a rise and fall of near-Edenic scale. So very much was gained in such short time—and nearly all was lost. The story of the city's survival, despite a near complete decimation of the social and economic underpinnings that supported it, is indeed a magnificent mystery. This is the kind of mystery Savannah-born author Flannery O'Connor referred to when she quoted St. Cyril of Jerusalem, who wrote: "The dragon sits by the side of the road, watching those who pass. Beware lest he devour you." No matter what form the dragon may take, O'Connor goes on to explain, "it is of this mysterious passage past him, or into his jaws, that stories of any depth will always be concerned to tell."[20] The houses and gardens depicted and described in the following pages bear silent witness to Savannah's miraculous passage past the dragons of time and change.

Manners and Modes of Living

In this same essay, O'Connor also talks about manners, noting that Southerners tend "to observe [their] fierce but fading manners in the light of an ultimate concern."[21] This concern, she explains, stems from the fear that their distinctly regional ways are in danger of being lost as the world becomes more ill-behaved and homogeneous. In speaking of manners, O'Connor refers not so much to the rules of politeness, but much more

According to John Berendt, author of Midnight in the Garden of Good and Evil*, antiques dealer Jim Williams transformed Mercer House "into something greater than its former grandeur." (Photograph by Herb Pilcher, October 20, 1979, Savannah Morning News)*

broadly to the defining characteristics of the inhabitants of a specific region. In both their unconscious adherence to age-old rules of etiquette and their very conscious efforts to preserve and interpret the various modes of living shaped by previous generations of their city's people, Savannahians and their homes are deeply informed by manners.

By 1833, Savannah was already gaining a reputation for politeness. "I admire these Savannah people more than any people I ever saw," wrote a visitor that year. "There is a great deal of wealth for a place so unpretentious. Everybody must be in easy circumstances, for everybody takes life easy. The ladies have a natural loveliness and grace, an ease of manner and self-possession, soft and gentle ways. And the gentlemen! They are so courteous and chivalrous in their bearing, so deferential to the ladies."[22] In *Gone with the Wind*, Margaret Mitchell described Savannah as "that gently mannered city by the sea." Once the war she chronicled had ended, these polite ways remained. Visiting journalist W.D. Howell remarked upon them in his 1919 essay, describing "those good manners which all men seem to have in Savannah, or for that matter the whole South in comparison with our Northern unceremoniousness."[23]

But fine manners were not always a given in Savannah, especially during its early periods of wealth, as this amusing 1818 description of nouveaux riches makes clear. "At four o'clock dinner was announced. Our platters were changed seven times and wine glasses five. At the head of the table was a large flat chicken pie, which the lady of the house informed us was made by one of the best French cooks in America and that it cost four dollars; at the foot of the table, a ham, which Mr. C informed us cost three times as much as American hams. At every new decanter, a fresh recommendation of its delicacy, with its price was given us. What a waste of money!"[24]

While some Savannahians may have acquired decorum somewhat later than citizens of more established capitals of commerce and culture, their descendants protected these polite ways fiercely as the material trappings of wealth and position began to slip away. Even the physical remains of Savannah's greatest wealth and architectural extravagance, which in their time might have bordered on the excessive and showy, appear more mannerly now that they have attained the patina of age. Whether they quietly continue to practice the customs and lifestyles of their ancestors or

French writer Julien Green, grandson of Charles Green, described the overwrought grandeur of the Green-Meldrim House as "splendid in a manner that seems peculiar to the Southern states."
(Photograph from the collection of the Library of Congress, courtesy of Historic Savannah Foundation)

creatively reinterpret them, present-day Savannahians invoke the manners of the past through their surroundings in a variety of ways, as the homes and gardens pictured in the following pages make clear.

Some Savannahians live in unbroken continuity with the past, surrounded by the same objects and, in some cases, even the same walls that accommodated their ancestors. Eight generations of the same family have inhabited Wormsloe, a plantation located just beyond the city's limits, which was among the original land grants of the Georgia colony. There, tabby foundations laid by one of Savannah's first settlers, avenues of oaks planted by one of his descendants, and Asian-inspired wall coverings installed by yet another family member reveal the various ways in which each generation has lived upon the place. At Lebanon Plantation, another of Georgia's original land grants, three generations of a family have inhabited a simple 19th-century frame house, adding rooms and outbuildings and redecorating them to suit their changing needs and lifestyles. At Comer House in downtown Savannah, the family who purchased it during the 1970s restoration movement has engaged in a decades-long scavenger hunt for the original decorative details and furnishings that ornamented it in the late 19th century. They have retrieved Victorian overmantels, wooden shutters, and even chairs with plush velvet upholstery tattered, but intact, in their effort to recreate the setting enjoyed by the home's first inhabitants.

Some Savannahians create simulations of traditional interiors—consciously imitative environments that invoke the spirit of the past without necessarily using objects that trace their provenance to old Savannah homes. One antiques dealer created a theatrical environment which celebrates Savannah's Eurocentric decadence, using French, English, and Italian antiques that he purchased during buying trips abroad. In a *pied-à-terre* above his antiques shop, he arranged these in playful vignettes that serve more as backdrops for occasional entertainments than practical settings for day-to-day living. In a Tybee Island beach cottage, an interior designer translated his childhood memories of summers spent at this popular Savannah retreat into three-dimensional reality. Using a hodgepodge of inherited and purchased furnishings, as well as decorative items including old wicker and bamboo, plastic tiki lights and colorful chenille bedspreads, he has created an inviting

interior that appears to have evolved through decades of family living, not a few years of purposeful design.

Instead of recreating an entire manner of living, some Savannahians select a single, essential aspect of regional style to celebrate and creatively reinterpret in their homes. An architect and his wife chose to explore the theme of eclecticism in their Greek Revival house. Just as Savannahians in the past tended to mix and match furnishings in the most up-to-date styles with cherished heirlooms reflecting older tastes, so has this couple blended modernist furnishings like Barcelona chairs and Parsons tables with American antiques. A young designer picked up the thread of Southern eccentricity when decorating his graceful Federal home. He suspended chandeliers designed for garden use from the ceiling medallions of his formal entertaining rooms, ornamented a pair of bull's-eye mirrors with halos of porcupine quills and decorated his bedroom with bizarre Masonic paraphernalia.

All of these homes, in their infinite diversity, are authentic expressions of Savannah style. Stymied by the city's aesthetic complexities, a visitor from Paris in 1934 described one of its grandest mansions, the Green-Meldrim House, as "both hideous and magnificent . . . semi-Gothic, semi-Louis XV." Yet ultimately he concluded that "[t]he whole thing remains splendid in a manner that seems peculiar to the Southern states."[25] These last words also aptly describe the entire city of Savannah—a splendid place that in its mysteries and manners remains entirely true to the peculiar character of the American South. But even within the larger region of the South, Savannah remains incomparable—unmatched in the integrity of its urban design, in its specific range of architectural expression and its particular blend of Old and New South style and spirit. "For the indescribable charm about its streets and buildings, its parks and squares…there is but one Savannah," declared an English clergyman in 1885, using words that ring as true today as they did more than one hundred years ago. "Without a rival, without an equal, it stands unique."[26]

Shades of the Past

The Comer House
Home of Edward and Caroline Hill

above: An overgrown garden replete with eerie statuary grows in the shadows of the house.

right: The sinuous silhouette of the side porch on this Italianate mansion reveals an exotic Moorish influence.

"The house is handsome and nicer than I ever dreamed of and when I entered it for the first time it looked very cheerful and I felt at home at once," wrote Lilla Comer to her grandmother in 1880, describing the new home her husband had prepared for her in Savannah, Georgia. "I had not the least idea it was so elegant…and found my good husband had deceived me in regard to it, having given me to understand that it was very plain and common."

"The carpets and furniture selected in New York are very handsome," Comer wrote in another letter. "The mantles are the handsomest I ever saw in my life. The Parlor furniture is ebony upholstered in raw silk and plush. There is a…bookcase in the sitting room. And a large Turkish rug before the fireplace in each room. Of course there are wanting many things in the way of draperies, bric-a-brac etc. but we shall get these things by degree and be in no hurry."

With the exception of these final details, Comer's letter still perfectly describes the house her husband built on Monterey Square, which has been lovingly restored and refurnished to period by its current owners, Ed and Caroline Hill. "We've done everything we could to preserve it exactly as it was," they explain. This twenty-year project has involved an elaborate treasure hunt in which the Hills have had to assume the roles of hunter, gatherer, archeologist, clairvoyant, and restoration contractor. The final result is a warm, inviting home that is simultaneously evocative of the past and resonant with present life.

Fortunately, the huge four-story Italianate house was in excellent condition when the Hills, proponents of the downtown restoration movement, purchased it in 1978. Original resident Lilla Comer had lived there for fifty-four years, long after her husband, New South industrialist, railroad president, mill owner, and rancher, Hugh Moss Comer, died in 1900. According to family history, she kept it exactly as it was in her husband's life for thirty-plus years

after his death. A Comer descendant who had visited in the
1930s claims that the house, as restored by the Hills, looks
and even smells just as it did back then.

Like many downtown homes, the Comer house was
turned into a rental property in the mid-1900s, but no
major structural changes were made during that time
except for kitchen and bath additions, subsequently
removed. Fortunately, many of the original decorative
details survived undamaged, including the elaborate
Renaissance Revival ceiling moldings in the formal rooms,
wood parquet floors, and the encaustic tiles in the stair hall.
Unfortunately, the elaborate overmantels that Lilla Comer
described and the fireplaces' decorative tile surrounds had
disappeared. Other missing elements included etched glass
and mahogany pocket doors, the front doors, and an iron
fence that once enclosed the spacious side garden. Even the
door knobs were missing on one floor, which had been
occupied for several years by a tenant with a hook hand.

The house itself seemed to play an active role in its
restoration, according to the Hills. "Every time we came across
a problem," Caroline Hill recalls, "the pieces would magically
reappear." Sometimes one of a pair of absent elements would
emerge from a dark corner in the basement or attic, providing
the Hills with a prototype to copy. Many missing pieces,
including doors, shutters, and the front parlor's overmantel
were found in a warehouse crammed with architectural
debris. "We could tell immediately if something was from this
house and we would buy it on the spot," Ed Hill declared. The
Hills even managed to buy back some of the original Comer
furniture, including a set of parlor chairs still upholstered in
the crimson silk plush Mrs. Comer used a century ago.

These original pieces are mixed and matched with a
collection of period furnishings that the Hills have inherited
and collected over the years. When they couldn't locate
replacements for the original Minton tiles used in the

*A large mirror reflects Renaissance Revival ceiling moldings and a
ghostly portrait painted by the Hills' daughter, Elsie.*

Gilded sphinxes supervise the comings and goings in the dark stair hall.

fireplaces, they photocopied images of them and taped them into place. Finding curtains that complemented the double parlor's time-worn opulence temporarily posed a problem, but eventually the Hills discovered old velvet draperies in a faded shade of amber at a nearby house sale. Though Caroline Hill prefers her windows bare, she settled upon an elaborate set of vintage striped silk swags discovered in an Atlanta antique shop for the formal front parlor. Period light fixtures range from a bronze argand chandelier to a converted gasolier in the form of twin sphinxes that makes an eerily ornate statement in the entrance hall.

The Hills describe their house as "the last of the old style houses to be built in Savannah." They are referring to the traditional arrangement of rooms running parallel along a side hall and to the home's severe Italianate facade. In fact, the house is transitional in style blending the Italianate taste, which dominated Savannah homes in the 1860s, with later Aesthetic movement influences including the use of English decorative tile, dark-carved chimney pieces and overmantels, and heavy ceiling and cornice moldings. While many of his contemporaries were opting for more modish architecture in the Queen Anne and Romanesque Revival styles, the 43-year old Hugh Comer selected a conservative compromise in the home he created for his second wife, a Connecticut Yankee.

Among other attractions, it was the home's Italianate flavor that appealed to the Hills. "We love everything Italian," they exclaim. Certainly, this is evident in the garden they have designed with its series of symmetrical rooms featuring classically inspired sculpture, gravel walks, and a rectangular *canopus*. But a distinct Victorian eclecticism creeps in even here, where a bronze sphinx crouches amid green foliage beneath the eaves of a porch detailed with Moorish railings. The Hills first painted this porch white, "trying to go with a Greek Revival look," they explain. "But

A spooky, 19th-century copy of Allesandro Allore's "Judith Holding the Head of Holfernes" greets visitors to the guest bedroom.

the house didn't like it," they add, insisting that it seemed to demand rich, dark, Umbrian tones within and without.

This somewhat brooding quality attracted the eye of film scouts searching for locations to use in filming *Midnight in the Garden of Good and Evil*. These scouts chose the Hills' house as the site for an early scene when John Cusack, playing John Berendt, arrives in Savannah and is greeted by his hostess who calls from the piazza, "What'll you have to drink?" They also selected the guest bedroom as the perfect location for a scene featuring eccentric Savannahian, Serena Dawes. The last room to undergo restoration in the Comer-Hill House, this bed/sitting room was redecorated in under two weeks in preparation for a day of filming.

The gold-patterned wallpaper and heavy scarlet draperies installed by Academy Award-winning production designer Henry Bumstead provide a perfect backdrop for the Hills' collection of heavy Empire furniture and a spooky 19th-century copy of Allesandro Allore's painting of "Judith Holding the Head of Holfernes." This sinister image, hung so prominently in the home's best guest room, seems to pay homage to the violent Gothic vein that runs through Southern history and literature, as defined by Edgar Allen Poe, William Faulkner, Flannery O'Connor, and more recently, temporary Southerner John Berendt.

Yet to the Hills, this house, with its darkly curving wooden ornaments, burnished tones of crimson and gold, and occasional sphinx and caryatid, is not an eerie place. It feels as cheerful and homelike to them as it did to Lilla Comer when she entered it as a new bride more than one hundred years ago. For Mrs. Comer, the home's ornate chiaroscuro epitomized the most fashionable taste of their time. For 21st-century Savannahians like the Hills, this play of light and shadow, at once opulent and vaguely ominous, evokes the complex spirit of the fallen, but unvanquished South.

A bronze sphinx crouches amid the overgrowth of the small Italianate garden.

Remembrance of Things Past
The Knapp House

Coils of plaster unfurl like fiddlehead ferns on the ceilings of all three entertaining rooms in the Knapp House, a high-style Greek Revival dwelling in Jasper Ward. Shimmering chandeliers with tier upon tier of faceted pendants and etched glass shades cascade like frozen waterfalls from elaborately modeled plaster rosettes in the center of each room. Lavish cornice moldings combining foliated shields with lacy borders cling with the tenacity of intertwining vines to the top of the walls. In the front parlor, elaborate gilt crowns of leaves and twisted braid surmount four, tall windows and a towering pier mirror. In the back parlor, real vines penetrate the window frames, forming organic ornamentation that invites inquiry regarding the relationship of art, imitation, and life.

Inhabitants with less self-possession or personal style than the current resident might easily be oppressed by such surroundings, cast into a state of meek subservience by the insistent grandeur of the interior or tempted into a stance of presumptuous competition. But the present owner felt immediately at home when he toured the property for the first time in 1963. "I could imagine my furniture in place, what color the walls would be, where my engravings would hang," he recalls. "I knew it was meant to be."

Perhaps it was his intimacy with the harp, that most stately and ornate of instruments, that cultivated such a sense of ease with these grandiose environs. "There has never been a day in my living memory when I did not know that the harp was my destiny," the owner says. A graduate from the University of Virginia with a degree in architecture, he spent three years in the Navy and used his mustering out money to buy his first harp. Invited to play as a guest performer in the Savannah Symphony in 1953, he moved to the city three years later to become a full-time harpist. Before moving to Savannah, the current resident of the Knapp House studied the harp and decorative arts in

*Elaborate moldings cling like overgrown vegetation to the walls and
ceilings of this high style Greek Revival mansion.*

Paris. This may explain why, although he grew up in north Georgia surrounded by American Empire furniture, his taste "strays to the French." A plenitude of Piranesi engravings suggests a classical influence as well, while Asian ceramics and prints of ancient Egyptian monuments reveal an underlying eclecticism. To all of these influences the owner brings his own unique sense of style to create a deeply personal, thoroughly lived and warmly hospitable domain.

"A bucket of paint and a bolt of fabric," is one of the owner's favorite ways to describe his approach to decoration. "At present, the bucket of paint is African Grass," he says as he stands in the front parlor, which has not been repainted in 35 years. "It's a nasty olive green or, if you want to be a bit nicer, a mustardy olive. It appears like it's been there forever and everything looks wonderful against it." The bolt of fabric is mattress ticking, made into pleated curtains that are surprisingly compatible with the ornate gilt cornice boards beneath which they hang. This seemingly unlikely choice of fabric brings to mind the Southern tradition of "summerizing" formal rooms by enveloping furniture in slipcovers of ticking. Possibly referring to such unintentional lapses into regional tradition, the owner muses about "the persistence of an unconscious memory" as a prevailing feature in Southern decoration and life style.

"In 1971, we had a 100th-birthday party for Marcel Proust in this house," he adds, without really changing the subject. "We served tea and madeleines, and when the tea and madeleines were done we had cocktails. It was a rather recherché group of people." In the middle parlor, Proust is celebrated in an abstract collage inscribed with the words "I love Marcel Proust" created by a long-time friend who also contributed two other drawings on Proustian themes.

When the owner was cogitating over the correct shade of mauve to paint his dining room in 1981, he came across a letter written by this same friend in which a paint chip labeled "choice mauvetone" was enclosed. On it the sender

The front doors are painted in hues that the resident describes as very Napoleon the Third.

Among other things, the resident collects blue and white Chinese porcelain, displayed here on a circa 1900 American sideboard.

had scribbled the cryptic words, "So hello! Save this for the non-believing." In order to explain the provenance of the room's striking color, the owner extracts this bit of ephemera from the seeming chaos of piles and stacks and heaps of things that covers nearly every horizontal surface in the house, proving beyond a shadow of a doubt that there is complete method to his organizational madness. Throughout the house, there are similar threads of abiding connectedness that unite apparently unrelated objects. "Most of these things have lived together for a long time," he says, indicating massive American Empire style furnishings passed down through generations of his family. "That Canton china belonged to the people who owned this house from 1909 to 1946," he points out, referring to a number of blue and white serving pieces that are aligned on the dining room's marble mantel.

The china was given to him by the daughter of Dr. Eugene Corson, a pioneering radiologist who may have taken one of the first X-ray photographs in America in the house's basement. "I am connected to more nice people through this house," says the owner, who loves to relate stories about the previous inhabitants. Combining an austere Greek Revival exterior with elaborate interior decoration, the house is attributed to master architect John Norris, who also designed the Green-Meldrim house and other ornate antebellum Savannah residences. The house was built in 1858 for Noah Knapp, a prosperous hardware merchant who had business interests in both the North and South. "Knapp survived the war better than most due to what we can call dual nationality," explains the owner, adding that "he had a daughter who died tragically young." He goes on to recount a story about a maid who swooned at the sight of the daughter's wedding dress laid out upon a bed. When she was roused, she accurately predicted, "Miz Knapp will never live to wear that gown!"

Otherworldly manifestations are apparently not uncommon in the house where an Episcopal priest once

The resident found the large wicker chairs at a sidewalk junk shop. He now enjoys them in his dining room, where he believes they deflate any possibility of pomposity.

"felt the presence" and saw a fingerless ghost wandering about the rooms. But more often than not, the visitors who frequent its rooms are flesh and blood. The owner, who loves to entertain, says that the house works wells for anywhere from two to 60 people. When his mother shared the house with him for more than fifteen years, the two enjoyed hosting entertainments including Thanksgiving dinner for a group of friends known as "the family" who were related by choice, not blood. "We had a table that could extend to seat fourteen," says the owner, who lately prefers dinner parties for six or so friends. "The best measurement of a good party is when the candles gutter and the conversation at table is still going strong."

Along with coveted recipes for blue cheese spread and roast lamb with chutney butter, candlelight is one of the key ingredients of a New Year's Eve party that has been hosted in the house for more than 40 years. Although she died ten years ago, "Mother is a part of this event still," says the owner, "very much like the Queen Mother." During the party, the house is lit by nothing but candles. "One of the great things about candles is that, when placed properly, they cast strategic shadows upon the dust," says the owner, who fantasizes about having a motto pillow embroidered with the words, "Dust waits." More reverently, he describes the quality his home acquires in the light of eighty glowing candles and a buzzing crowd of guests: "I become an outsider, a dispassionate onlooker watching as the house takes on a life of its own, becoming magical and alive."

"You'll never know how beautiful this house is until you see it filled with people having a good time," Dr. Corson's daughter told the owner the day he bought the house. Fortunately, he lives with this beauty daily, whether surrounded by the company of friends or shades of former residents whose presence ornaments the rooms as tangibly as the architectural details that decorate the walls and ceilings in rich, timeworn relief.

The blue Canton china belonged to the family who lived in the house in the first decades of the 20th century and was given to the current occupant by a descendant.

A Sacred Trust

The Champion, Harper-Fowlkes House Headquarters of the Society of the Cincinnati in the State of Georgia

above: The monumental portico of this Greek Revival mansion is nearly obscured by a pair of massive magnolia trees that are protected by the will of the house's preserver and protector, Alida Harper Fowlkes.

right: This center hall is one of the grandest in Savannah, with its marble parquet, faux-marble columns and pilasters, and elliptical oculus through which a chandelier once hung.

High-stakes finance, sudden bankruptcy, properties lost, recovered, and preserved, pride of place and a deep sense of stewardship characterize the history of the Champion, Harper-Fowlkes House and reflect the mercurial fortunes of the city that it graces. The house's story began in 1842 when Stephen Gardner, partner in the thriving shipping firm of Samuel Philbrick & Company, decided to build a mansion on Orleans Square. He borrowed $5,000 from his brother and ordered building materials from Henry McAlpin, a brick manufacturer whose home and factory were located at the Hermitage outside of town. Within a year, Gardner's company had failed. He was forced to sell his home to his brother and faced charges from McAlpin who was suing to recover the cost of the building materials.

Three months later, the unfinished house found a new owner, "an enterprising and successful business man" named Aaron Champion. "[I]n 1861," according to a history written about the house, "he was elected President of the Marine Bank and Fire Insurance Company of Savannah, a position which he held until the bank was liquidated after the Civil War. It was one of the few banks to survive that trying period, perhaps because (according to legend) hearing that Sherman's troops were headed for Savannah, Champion concealed the bank's gold in the well [of his house]. Then after the war, he retrieved it all but one $10.00 gold piece!"[1] It is presumed that the well-financed Champion completed the construction and interior detailing of the mansion, an imposing Greek Revival structure that is attributed to Charles McCluskey, one of Savannah's most important mid-nineteenth century architects.

Situated on a trust lot overlooking Orleans Square, the house seems to soar upward from the ground, an illusion created by a massive two-story portico supported by Corinthian columns set between two square corner piers. Built of McAlpin's Savannah grey brick, the house received

a coat of stucco, which was scored to resemble heavy stone blocks. The interior of the house is as imposing as its facade. A wide center hall paved with blue and white marble squares provides a stately first impression. Four square columns rise in the middle of this space, supporting a ceiling panel pierced by an eliptical oval through which light shines from a skylight above. Originally, a chandelier suspended from the attic hung down through this opening.

Four large rooms open off this dramatic hall: three spacious sitting rooms and a luxurious dining room. Plaster moldings of varying intricacy crown these high-walled chambers and gold leaf window cornices and matching pier mirrors accent two of the rooms. Hanging from the ceilings are gilded gasoliers, eleborately ornamented fixtures produced by the Cornelius Company of Philadelphia. The Champion, Harper-Fowlkes House is one of the very few houses of this era to boast six such gasoliers. Even more remarkable is the fact that these fixtures, considered to be little more than scrap metal in the early 20th century, still remain in place and in near perfect condition.

Despite their rich ornamentation, three of the four entertaining rooms have a light and airy feel, contributed in part by the generous placement of tall windows and the high ceilings. Against the backdrop of light-colored plaster walls, a collection of American Empire and English furniture is arranged in parlors that have a distinct air of decorum and restraint. These rooms reflect the taste of Alida Harper Fowlkes, the house's ninth owner and its protector and preserver. But the dining room reveals the more exuberant style of the house's late-19th-century inhabitants.

By 1895, Aaron Champion's grandchildren were living in the house which they decided to remodel in the fashionable Second Empire baroque manner. While they left the front portico unaltered, they added an entire third floor, accommodated beneath a mansard roof, and a glazed cupola that brought natural light into the center of the house. Maria Champion McAlpin and her husband also relocated the interior stairs to the back of the house in order to create a large dining room, which they decorated with faux-bois surfaces. These painted and glazed walls and ceiling, considered by experts to be some of the best of their period, were hidden until recently beneath a layer of wallpaper. When workers accidentally destroyed a panel of wallpaper, they revealed the glowing amber surface, which has now been fully revealed and preserved by the present owners of the house.

Details of the property's wrought-iron fence and curved stair can be glimpsed through ivy-clad tree trunks.

The dining room, with its brilliantly gleaming gilt detail and richly decorative wall treatments, attests to the opulent taste of well-to-do late-19th-century Savannahians. Sadly, the soaring prosperity that financed this lavish life style did not last long into the twentieth century. Like many of their neighbors, the last generation of McAlpins to live in the house sold their ancestral home in the 1930s. By that time, many of downtown Savannah's grand homes and townhouses had been abandoned, demolished, or converted into tenements. Unwieldy mansions on corner lots were among the first buildings to succumb to the wrecking ball. But the Champion, Harper-Fowlkes House was rescued from that fate by Mrs. Fowlkes, an antiques dealer and an ardent preservationist who purchased it in 1939 for $9,000, the lowest price it had ever attained.

Described by architectural historian Roulhac Toledano as "a rugged individualist and antiques dealer," Mrs. Fowlkes rescued a total of eight Savannah houses, including the Georgian style Pink House where she operated a tea shop in the 1930s. According to Fowlkes's friend, Margaret "Peg" Fuller, she passed by the old McAlpin house each day on her way to the City Market to buy vegetables and vowed, "Some day I will own that house." Once she succeeded in buying it, Mrs. Fowlkes modified it slightly, without destroying the integrity of the interior, and decorated it in the style of mid-19th-century Savannahians, using family antiques and furnishings she collected on annual buying trips for the antiques store she operated on Madison Square. She lived in the house she had admired since childhood for the remainder of her years.

When she neared the end of her life, Mrs. Fowlkes sought a way to protect the house in perpetuity and to keep her decorations and furniture intact so that future generations might appreciate the period lifestyle she had so carefully evoked. An ardent steward of Savannah's architecture and decorative arts, she looked for a new steward who would not only preserve the house but also enjoy using it through the years. At last, she settled upon not a single person, but an entire and august organization: the Society of the Cincinnati in the State of Georgia, comprised of descendants of the officers who fought under George Washington in the Revolutionary War. In January 1985, she died, leaving the house in trust to the Society, for use as its headquarters, as well as the lion's share of her estate, "to use the net income for the maintenance, upkeep and operation of the said home."

Richly painted walls and ceilings and intricate gilt gasoliers reveal the lavish tastes of the house's late-19th-century inhabitants.

The elaborate faux-bois of the dining room was revealed only recently when a fragment of wallpaper was removed.

Mrs. Fowlkes also left a detailed will filled with specific instructions regarding the care and interpretation of the house, including prohibitions against cutting down the trees that now obscure the front portico. Long before her death, she hand-picked members and associates of the society to supervise any changes that might be made to the house, including her brother, Colonel William B. Harper, Jr.; life-long friend, Mrs. Hunter M. "Eleanor" Clay; Mrs. Fuller; and several others. "She opened drawers and showed us things in the collection and agreed that we might have to move a few of the furnishings in order to accommodate large groups of people," Mrs. Fuller recalls. "She had wonderful taste and she knew it, and she wanted us to leave the house as much as possible the way it had always been."

Today, the silver still sits upon the sideboards in the dining room as it did in Mrs. Fowlkes's day. The Society's members gather regularly in the house to discuss their patriotic activities, as well as those related to the preservation and restoration of the property, such as the demolition of a filling station built on the land and the creation of a walled garden and a carriage house. Members of the organization use the house frequently for elegant social occasions, including receptions and coming-out parties, and make it available periodically to the Savannah Tour of Homes, which raises funds for ongoing preservation city-wide. "We consider the house a sacred trust," says Mrs. Fuller, making clear that this grand house will long survive to tell the stories of the people who have shaped its history, just as Mrs. Fowlkes planned that it should.

This double parlor reflects Mrs. Fowlkes's efforts to recreate the mid-19th-century appearance of these rooms.

overleaf: The exquisitely appointed rooms of the Champion, Harper-Fowlkes House
seem to wait in a perpetual state of anticipation for the return of long-gone occupants.

Champion, Harper Fowlkes House   45

A Slightly Faded Grandeur

The Thomas Levy House
Home of John and Ginger Duncan

John and Ginger Duncan are drawn irresistibly to old maps, prints, and books. The creamy gold of aging paper, rich tones of printer's inks, and mysterious subjects portrayed, whether unknown lands, unfamiliar birds, or unfurling flowers, work a peculiar magic upon them. Ginger prefers maps while John favors prints. Books are a mutual obsession. The spoils of their international collecting sprees provide inventory for the Old Curiosity Shop-like establishment they operate at the northeast corner of Monterey Square. Announced by a discreet sign advertising antique maps, prints and books, the shop occupies the first floor of the Duncans' Taylor Street home. The style and contents of the living quarters above share much in common with the rare printed matter below: the golden hue of age enriched with jewel tones here and there, the discrimination of avid and informed collectors, and the idiosyncratic taste of uncompromising individuals.

The flamboyantly ornamented exterior of the house prepares visitors well for the opulence within. Built in 1869 in the Italianate manner, the house received an extensive remodeling in 1897 in the Second Empire baroque manner attributed to Beaux Arts-trained architect Detlef Lienau who introduced the highly decorative style to Savannah. In the wonderfully descriptive words of architectural historian Roulhac Toledano[1], "this excessive and fluid style applied to Savannah's staid English facades creates an amusing and fanciful street scene."

The remodeling, undertaken at the behest of prosperous Savannah merchant B. H. Levy, called for the addition of marble steps, projecting bays, a mansard roof, and extensive exterior ornamentation including a garlanded frieze, bracketed cornices, a gargoyle, and pedimented dormers. The result, with its multiple layers of white-on-white detail, looks like a big slice of wedding cake perched upon the city street. Within, the late 19th century restyling

above: A street level shop filled with antique maps, prints and books glows with the warm tones of aged paper, leather, and wood.

left: Second Empire baroque details embellish this Italianate townhouse to create a highly decorative, fanciful facade.

The marble mantel in the front parlor dates from the 1869 construction of the house, while the gilt cornices, pier mirror, gasolier, and stenciled ceilings reflect the more exuberant tastes of late-19th-century residents.

lends an air of undeniable extravagance to rooms that previously exhibited more mid-century restraint. Massive gilt cornices in the Renaissance Revival style crown the front parlor's tall windows and frame an equally colossal pier mirror. Above, the ceiling is decorated with wreaths of flowers and ribbons stenciled upon a tawny field. Twenty-four years ago, the Duncans removed the wallpaper from the ceiling to reveal the delicate detail. "Much of the pattern came down with the wallpaper," John recalls, "and a good bit of the wallpaper paste remained." At first the Duncans were disappointed with the effect, but they came to admire it so much that they hired an artist to faux-finish the walls to match. "We spent a lot of money to make it look like we'd spent no money," John adds in a wry aside.

During the 1890s restyling, pocket doors separating the front parlor and dining room were replaced with a broken arch to create a sweeping suite of rooms. Elaborate gilt gasoliers, since converted to electricity, lit the rooms and matching marble fireplaces provided heat. Today, colorful Oriental carpets cover the floors, including a Saraband purchased for $1 from the condemned DeSoto Hotel. Local paintings and rare prints adorn the walls, including aquatints from Audubon's famous double elephant folio depicting Savannah Finches with Indian Pink-Root and Warbling Flycatchers on a Swamp Magnolia. Sculpture ranging in scale from the near-life-size Native American by Charleston artist Willard Hirsch to bronze figurines of George Washington and John C. Calhoun stand at attention.

The private rooms above, though more intimate and less formal, are just as rich in color, contents, and detail as the impressive entertaining rooms below. A stately marble mantel ornamented with Ionic pilasters dominates one wall of the decidedly masculine master bedroom up one flight of stairs. The Duncans brought the mantel, which originally

This detail from the front door reveals the delicate classicism employed by Beaux Arts-trained Detlef Lienau, to whom the house's 1897 remodeling is attributed.

graced a bedroom in Charleston's Sword Gate House, in the back of their station wagon to Savannah. "The previous owner didn't like waking up to all that dark marble," John notes. Here, the black and gold marble inspired the room's entire color scheme and the stylized lotus motif of its tile surround is repeated in a frieze painted by a local artist around the room's high walls.

According to oral history, the four-poster bed in this room once graced Lyndhurst, robber baron Jay Gould's Hudson River estate. It subsequently provided a retreat for Helen Drexel, inspiration for the character Serena Dawes in *Midnight in the Garden of Good and Evil* and a real-life Savannah socialite described in a 1939 article from the *Woman's Home Companion* as a "Yachting Enthusiast . . . and Belle of Masquerade." "Helen lived in that bed with her French poodle, Lulu," John confides. "She seldom left it even while giving parties."

Beyond the faux-grained bedroom door lies a room that can only be described as the heart of the house. The small study throbs with an antiquarian's passion for old books and *objéts*. Floor-to-ceiling bookshelves cover two walls—one dedicated to South Carolina (John is a 12th-generation Charlestonian) and the other, to Georgia (he is also a former history professor and frequent lecturer on local history and architecture). High up on a freestanding bookcase, an 1880s plaster copy of the Parthenon's Horse of Selene tosses its mane in challenge to any who dare enter this inner sanctum. John tells a particularly amusing story involving bribery and an excursion to a ravine that explains, in a round-about way, how the horse's head ended up in his library. The Staffordshire figurine of Benjamin Franklin standing on the desk sparks another delightful aside. "If you look closely, you'll see that it is labeled 'George Washington,'" John points out. "We know far more about the English than they know about us," he gravely

An earthenware jar holds a collection of walking sticks carved and painted by two generations of African-Americans from the Pinpoint, Georgia area.

Savannah socialite Helen Drexel is rumored to have presided over house parties from this antique bed. The chest of drawers, circa 1828–29, is signed by Boston cabinet maker Rufus Pierce.

adds. Another $1 carpet from the DeSoto Hotel warms the floor and an oversized Chippendale reproduction chair provides an appropriately larger-than-life seat for its imposing six-foot, seven-inch tall owner.

Although compared to her husband, Ginger is diminutive in stature, she matches him in wit as well as enthusiasm for their shared domain. Drawn to the then dilapidated house by an advertisement describing it as "partially restored," Ginger describes their relationship to it as love at first sight, adding that her mother burst into tears when she first saw it. But with a price tag of $36,000 and a location on Monterey Square—which the Duncans insist is the prettiest in Savannah—they were willing to undertake the task of restoration, which is still underway twenty-five years later. "The Levys spent $4,000 remodeling the house in 1897," Ginger is fond of saying. "We have spent considerably more and done considerably less."

Fortunately, the Duncans share a passion for things that are rich with history and show their years. "I love the slightly faded grandeur of gilt with a little bit of paint remaining, not perfectly shining," exclaims John, referring to the cornices he hastily stripped one Saturday. He might as well be describing his entire home which does not brashly shine but gently gleams with the subtle patina of age.

Southern Light

The Mills House
Home of Richard and Audrey Platt

Many of Savannah's homes and gardens share a dark, mysterious air. Attached townhouses dwell in one another's shadows and tall garden walls enclose mossy courtyards that thrive in shade. Deep porches screen interior rooms from the harsh light of a semi-tropical sun. And heavy shutters, overhanging window moldings, and velvet draperies devour what little light dares intrude these sun-shy dwellings. But the Italianate house built on Hall Street in 1881 for Mr. and Mrs. George Mills, defies these tenebrous traditions. Rising four stories high with a mansard roof added in a Second Empire baroque remodeling, this gracious house welcomes the sun on all four sides.

Fronting a city street twice the usual width, the house's facade basks in southern light. Only a mammoth oak tree, nearly 300 years old and measuring twenty-three feet around at the base, filters the sun on the eastern, garden side. Decades ago, a two-story piazza encased this facade of the house, but over the years it decayed and collapsed. Rather than rebuild it, the present owners constructed a small balcony of cast iron that overlooks the garden without blocking the light. The garden itself is one of the largest in Savannah's Landmark District. When it was first laid out, the property abutted a second garden of equal size belonging to owner's sister who lived on the far side of the same city block.

The current owners chose the house for its bright, cheerful aspect and its elegantly appointed entertaining rooms, which feature white marble mantles handcrafted for the house in Italy, original moldings, and plaster ceiling medallions. The large and airy drawing room has a bay window on one side and floor-to-ceiling windows on another, which overlook the garden and open onto the gracious side balcony. Painted a soft, dove grey that contrasts subtly with the white plaster and woodwork, the room shows a refined eye for color and shape evident throughout the house. Striped French silk adorns an 1820

One of the largest private gardens in Savannah, this side yard encompasses a sunken terrace and reflecting pool, plantings of azaleas, cherry trees and ferns, and a massive live oak tree.

A subtle grisaille palette and restrained approach to decoration emphasize the fine proportions and elegant architectural details of the drawing room.

Delicate shadows cast by the ancient oak repeat the tracery of this cast iron balcony.

Empire sofa, reflecting the grey and white color scheme and adding a crisply tailored air. Transitional Louis XV–XVI arm chairs painted and upholstered in white flank the sofa, and on the walls above, a pair of stone-colored 19th-century Tole sconces with a lily design contribute a slightly deeper tone of grey. Against these cool shades the reds and browns of the wooden floor, the polished Pembroke tables, and the Oriental rugs glow with a welcome warmth.

In order to maintain a spare, almost modern feel in the room, the owners eschewed curtains, relying instead upon shutters to filter the strong sunlight, and chose not to hang a chandelier from the ceiling medallion. But in the adjoining dining room, the windows are luxuriously dressed in lemon-colored silk that cascades all the way down to the floor where it falls in bright puddles against the heart pine boards. Hanging from the room's intricate ceiling medallion is a delicate 18th-century, Dutch chandelier of ormolu which, when illuminated, casts a soft radiance on the French dining table below. Asian elements offer exotic notes in both rooms: a 17th century lacquered chest in black and burnished gold, a folding screen painted in the Oriental style by Savannah artist Christopher Murphy, a collection of Chinese export ware, and a tiny bonsai tree. Whimsical additions like a large tureen in the shape of a swan and a long-legged child's correctional chair from the Victorian period introduce surprising shapes and scale. Cherished antiques include a French *secrétaire abattant* signed by an 18th-century master of marquetry.

The grisaille color scheme continues in the entrance hall, which parallels the main entertaining rooms. Architectural elements including a bracketed arch, multi-layered crown moldings, and grooved wooden paneling add ornamental detail to this space. A large pier mirror anchors one wall, reflecting a mid-19th-century portrait by G. P. A. Healy of Nellie Kinzie, the owner's grandmother

and mother of Girl Scouts of America founder, Juliette
Gordon Low. Posed in a full-skirted satin gown, the
subject seems to be gazing at her reflection before stepping
out the front door for an evening's entertainment.
Victorian chairs in the Gothic style and a pair of 18th-
century Venetian mirrored sconces add even more
decorative interest to this entrance hall.

Despite the loving placement of family antiques and
reverence for historic architecture demonstrated throughout
this home, the owners' aesthetic is clearly informed by a
spare and modern sensibility. Nowhere is this inclination
more obvious than in a contemporary kitchen addition they
created several years ago, an atriumlike space attached to the
rear of the house. But in the garden, which was little more
than an overgrown yard dominated by the gargantuan oak
and creeping ivy ten years ago, the Platts have remained
faithful to more traditional tastes. "We wanted to create a
garden that looked as though it had been here for hundreds
of years," they explain.

Working with Savannah garden expert Jim Morton, the
residents defined a hardscape of radiating circles and
rectangles paved with a variety of old bricks and stones in
shades of pink and grey. A circular bed of Asian jasmine
surrounds the ancient oak while an elliptical pool reflects its
branches in the corner of the lot. A sunken rectangular
garden that provides a secluded area for outdoor dining is
edged with ferns and white tulips, which bloom in a
luminous show each spring. Ten different varieties of ferns
supply a year-round backdrop of cascading shapes and
shades of green throughout the garden. White accents in the
form of blossoming cherry trees, azalea blooms, and calla
lilies offer pale contrast, intensified here and there with the
brighter shades of lavender azaleas and deep blue violas.

As the sun plays on the garden paths, it is hard to
imagine this neighborhood as anything other than a

pleasant, residential block. But the owners remember how
different the half-empty streets felt thirty years ago. "For the
first time in years, children and dogs were seen on the
sidewalks again," they recall, remembering the 1970s, when
young couples began moving back downtown during the
restoration movement. Reclaiming these grand properties
for themselves, these preservationist pioneers also restored
them to the city. Today, separated from the street by a low
iron fence salvaged from old St. Joseph's Hospital, the
garden can be enjoyed almost as much by passersby as the
residents themselves. And even though pedestrians won't
see the rooms inside of the house, they can still enjoy the
architectural elements that decorate its façade—elegant
embellishments that bespeak the wealth and glamour of a
time now past, but lovingly recalled.

Beauty and Strength

The Owens-Thomas House
A House Museum of the Telfair Museum of Art

At first glance, the Owens-Thomas House conveys an impression of robust stateliness. The rigorously symmetrical facade, standing tall and wide upon a raised basement, dominates the northeast trust lot overlooking Oglethorpe Square. Constructed of brick, natural cement and coquina with heavy quoins outlining the corners and a dentiled cornice wrapping around the whole, the building boldly asserts its strength and solidity. Upon closer inspection, however, the house's classically inspired ornamentation lends an air of delicacy which offsets with the grave solidity of the overall form. A serpentine entrance porch supported by tapering Ionic columns extends from the front of the house where it is approached by a pair of curving stairs with gracefully spiraling rails of iron. On the south facade, a cast-iron balcony displays an even more unrestrained decorative impulse. Reaching out over the fence that surrounds the lot, the balcony rests upon elaborate floral consoles which support four fluted Corinthian columns and a projecting anthemia cornice. While contributing to the overall impressiveness of the edifice, this balance of beauty and strength is also the key to the endurance of this home. America's finest English Regency style dwelling, the Owens-Thomas House has survived nearly two centuries of dramatic history which have witnessed the destruction or extreme alteration of nearly all other buildings designed in Savannah by its architect, William Jay.

This house was completed in 1819 during a golden age which began in Savannah following the War of 1812. "Peace with England in 1815 ended the economic hardships caused by embargoes and naval conflicts," writes Page Talbott in *Classical Savannah*, a volume cataloging the flourishing of decorative and fine arts in Savannah during the first half of the 19th century. "Savannah's merchants thrived anew, residential and commercial building projects were vigorously initiated, and local citizens faced the future

Although it was considered an innovative showpiece in Savannah, the Owens-Thomas House shares much in common with Regency buildings constructed in Bath and London.

with optimism and confidence."[1] In leaner times, the city's residents tended to construct simple wood frame dwellings that were susceptible to fire and decay, but during Savannah's intermittent economic booms, larger houses designed by sophisticated architects added variety and majesty to the city's streets.

Describing the cityscape in 1839, a visitor to Savannah wrote, "...there are many handsome and commodious brick buildings occupied as private residences, and a few mansions, built by an English architect, Mr. Jay...which are of beautiful architecture, of sumptuous interior, and combine as much of elegance, and luxury as are to be found in any private dwellings in the country."[2] Jay arrived in Savannah in 1817, having already received a commision in the city from Richard Richardson, who was related to him by marriage. Born in Bath in 1792, Jay had recently completed his apprenticeship under a London surveyor and architect during which he was exposed to the classical vocabulary of the English Regency style. He brought to the American city what architectural historian James Cox described as "a whole new bag of tricks that would considerably enhance the architectural scene."[3] These ranged from a fluency with ancient Greek and Roman forms, a familiarity with the spatial and decorative sophistication of late 18th and early 19th century architects including Robert Adam and John Soane and facility with emerging materials and technologies including cast iron construction and indoor plumbing.

Richard Richardson, a cotton broker, attorney and president of the Savannah branch of the Bank of the United States, engaged the precocious architect to design a showplace for him and his family on Orleans Square. This was to be the first, and many consider finest, of the public and private structures Jay designed in Savannah before returning to England in the wake of a severe economic

Classical elements abound in this small room, including the fluted pilasters on the marble mantel, the column depicted in the painting above, and the gilded form of the harp.

Curving lines of brass accentuate the graceful lines of the stair railings.

depression just a few years after he arrived. At the height of his fortune, Richardson commissioned Jay to design a mansion that would reflect both his own prosperity and the au courant tastes of London and Bath. Jay, eager to establish his reputation in Savannah, willingly complied, creating a house that was innovative in form and decoration and widely heralded as one of Savannah's most beautiful homes.

Jay's inventiveness is immediately impressed upon the visitor who enters the house from the portico, walking into a spectacular entrance hall dominated by a dramatic staircase. Framed by a pair of fluted columns with gilded Corinthian capitals and marble consoles (added after 1830) bearing busts of Lord Byron and Sir Walter Scott, the stairs ascend towards the back of the house in a single flight that divides at a landing into two flights. These flights return toward the front of the house, rising to the second floor where they rejoin to create an arched bridge that connects the front rooms of the house with those in the rear. The stairs' gleaming oak treads and graceful mahogany railings are inlaid with thin bands of brass that reflect the light and accentuate the intricate geometry of the structure. A cutwork frieze in the form of undulating waves runs along the edge of the stairs and cast iron balusters, originally treated with verdigris paint and powdered bronze gilding, add even further embellishment.

While it is hard to imagine that any other room in the house could compete with the visual excitement of this entrance hall, the entertaining rooms that lie on either side are equally surprising. To the right lies a drawing room where an artfully designed ceiling creates a trompe l'oeil effect. Although the room is fairly small and the ceiling, flat, the addition of a circular fret embellished in the Greek key pattern and fluted corner pendentives creates the impression of a large room surmounted by a domed ceiling. On either side of a marble mantle featuring classically draped figures

Plaster ceiling details, including a circular fret and fluted pendentives in each corner, create the illusion that this relatively small, square room is a circular space surmounted by a shallow dome.

are a pair of arched niches that provided the perfect place for the Richardson family to showcase items from their extensive collection of fine art and furniture. Although these possessions were dispersed in the early 19th century, today the room is decorated with fine American-made furniture including pieces from the workshops of Duncan Phyfe and a portrait by English artist and Jay's friend, William Etty.

Across the hall lies an equally lavish chamber, a dining room that has been described as "one of the most remarkable neoclassical interiors in America."[4] Here, Jay varied the rectangular form by creating a rounded bay at the far side of the room in which symmetrical curved doors open into a china closet in one corner and a connecting hallway in the other. Demilune openings rise over these doorways and above these, a free-standing cornice of plaster anthemia encircles the room with an intricate lace-like border. Jay avoided excessive fenestration in his structures, writing in 1819 that windows distracted from "that repose that is so essential in architecture." This preference is evident in the dining room, which has only two windows opening onto the front of the house (a third window was sealed up as a blind window during or soon after the original construction). In order to brighten the room without compromising his sense of design, Jay created a shallow niche in the long side wall over which he installed a curving projection fitted with amber glass and a screen ornamented with a Greek key pattern. Soft light filters through this novel architectural feature, illuminating a rare Regency serving table of marble and mahogany below.

Another unusual detail, added after 1830, adds colorful illumination to the second floor stair hall. French doors that enhance the flow of air and light into this space are outlined with sidelights glazed in cobalt blue and amber panes. Three ample bedrooms and a library share this floor, providing comfortable quarters for Richardson's family and

The Owens-Thomas House 75

their guests, quarters which included the uncommon luxury of indoor bathing and toilet facilities. Sadly, the Richardsons enjoyed their lavish home for only three years. In 1822, Richardson lost his wife to an untimely death and his fortune to a national depression which ruined many of Savannah's families and businesses. He was forced to relinquish the title of his house to his business partner. Soon afterwards it was leased to Mrs. Mary Maxwell who operated it as a refined boarding house for seven years. It was during this period that the Revolutionary War hero the Marquis de Lafayette made his tour of the South and stayed in the Richardsons' former home, which was selected as the most suitable accommodations for the returning hero. Lafayette delivered two public speeches from the house during his stay.

In 1830, the house was purchased by George Welchman Owens and remained in his family for three generations until, in 1951, his granddaughter, Miss Margaret Thomas left it and its contents to the Telfair Academy of Arts and Sciences, today known as the Telfair Museum of Art. She designated the house "in trust to be preserved, maintained and used as a museum in perpetuity for the benefit and use of the public as a memorial to [her] grandfather . . . and to [her] father…." The house, in its largely unaltered and excellently preserved condition, does serve as a monument to the careful custodianship of the Owens family and Telfair Museum. It also bears witness to the soaring ambitions of previous generations of Savannahians and the exquisite taste of the artisans they employed to translate their visions of new world prosperity into reality.

Despite the mercurial elements—economic, political and natural—that constantly altered the face and fortunes of the city, this house has survived thanks both to the solidity of its masonry construction and the winning beauty of its ornamentation. In his *Reminiscences and Recollections of Old Savannah*, published in 1928, Charles S. H. Hardee describes a series of devastations that struck the city in the year following the completion of the house, including a fire consuming nearly 500 houses, a severe storm and an epidemic of yellow fever. While the solidity of Jay's construction protected it against such physical threats, it was the house's beauty that defended it against the destructiveness of subsequent generations who wantonly demolished many other fine mansions or impatiently remodeled them in more modish styles. Like the Greek and Roman monuments that inspired its classical design, the Richardson-Owens-Thomas House stands slightly aloof from the throng of tourists and commercial traffic that fills the street beyond its doors, bearing silent witness to the staying power of great dreams and beautiful designs.

A Comfortable Place with No Pretension

Lebanon Plantation
Home of Mary and Howard Morrison

The road to Lebanon plantation seems not just to wind through the rural countryside outside Savannah but also to travel back through time. Veering off a two-lane highway, the dirt road passes through a long arcade of ancient oaks festooned with Spanish moss. Second-growth forest and old growing fields spread out as far as the eye can see on either side, hinting of the agricultural purposes this property served for more than two centuries. An old tenant house at the side of the road, with its shining tin roof and brick chimney, looks as though it might still be inhabited by a family of sharecroppers. A hundred or so yards further on, the road crosses a railroad track where trains still heave their loads of raw and manufactured goods to and from Savannah's port.

At the end of the road, the sun plays gently upon the remains of two, pierced brick walls mellowed a greyish-pink with age and a copse of old camellia trees. Beyond, a traditional plantation home of white clapboard raised upon a brick foundation stands high within a crescent of out-buildings. A simple stair leads to the land entrance, but a quick stroll around the side of the house allows visitors to approach the grander waterside facade of the house, which was designed to face the Little Ogeechee River. Early-19th-century visitors to Lebanon plantation traveled to the house along a path leading from a river dock through a forest to the grassy clearing that still provides a dramatic setting for the house. The house that James Habersham built in 1804, however, was a much simpler, smaller affair than the now-expansive compound, which has been added onto and embellished over the years. Early-20th-century photographs show a plain, two-story center-hall structure, which was intended more as a working plantation home than a luxurious country retreat.

The original design, with its raised basement and wrap-around, double galleries, is similar to that of plantation houses located along the rivers and bayous of Mississippi and

Lebanon Plantation started out as a simple two-story house with a dirt floor and a raised basement that was gradually expanded and embellished over the centuries.

Louisiana. During Mr. Habersham's day, Lebanon's primary crop was rice but when the plantation was first established in 1755 through a grant from King George II to James DeVeaux, it was expected to produce rice, indigo, and silk. Brick foundations at the edge of the river show where the original settlers lived as they experimented with crops. White mulberry trees of the type used for the cultivation of silkworms still grow on the property. A garden planted with more than a hundred species of camellias is a reminder that this country soil nurtured ornamental plants as well, including exotic trees and flowers that were carefully cultivated and traded among friends.

"[T]he Camellia plant exchanges that took place between plantation owners partook of the same flavor of rivalry that characterized their interest in houses and other animal breeds," surmised a scholar invited to catalog the plants on Lebanon's 1000 acres. Current owner Howard Morrison also identified Satsuma orange and Tung oil trees (a gift from Henry Ford) that hint at other agricultural endeavors in the early 20th century. Plantings of naturalized snowdrops and fragrant white narcissus reveal where walkways and carriage paths once laced the property, and old dikes and overgrown fields are evidence of the days when rice was the Low Country's most lucrative crop before the combined effects of Reconstruction and two devastating hurricanes ended its commercial viability in the late 19th century.

Two stories describing events that occured at Lebanon during the Civil War bring the lost plantation lifestyle back into vivid focus. The first took place before Savannah's surrender, when many wives were left to supervise plantation business while their husbands, fathers, and sons defended the interests of the Confederacy. At the time, Lebanon was in the possession of Major George Anderson, commander of Fort McAllister on the Great Ogeechee

The graceful classical forms of a hammered silver tea service dating from the 19th century gleams atop a Sheraton style sideboard.

River. During his absence, the house was ransacked by marauding Union troops. Using an old back road that connected Lebanon with the nearby Saranac Plantation, Mrs. Anderson sent her silver packing whenever Federal soldiers approached. As the troops drew near, she would calmly greet them from her porch and explain that all the silver was already stolen. Once they had finished searching the house for other valuables, she would send word to bring the silver back and enjoy tea served from her silver teapot, upholding the traditional formalities cherished by Southerners in wartime as well as peace.

The second story tells of Federal officers who were actually invited to dine at Lebanon and to drink and eat from its silver and crystal as terms of an honorable surrender negotiated by Major Anderson following the fall of Fort McAllister. As told in a story entitled "Enemies Drink a Toast",[1] Major Anderson discovered that the Commanding General of the Union Army assaulting the fort under his command was a former friend and comrade-at-arms. This fact emboldened him to suggest unusual terms of surrender for himself and his men. "I then proposed to him that…the General and his staff come to my home at Lebanon plantation, and allow me and my officers to give a dinner in their honor," recounts the Major in this telling. "My men were to march out with the honors of war and be paroled….Our silver and wines were brought back from secret hiding places and…[t]oasts were drunk to my defense of Fort McAllister and to the brave men under my command, and the party broke up with an exchange of felicitations from both sides."

Unfortunately, the years following the South's defeat proved less felicitous for the Andersons, who were forced to sell their property. Lebanon was ultimately purchased by Mills B. Lane, founder of the Citizens & Southern Banks in Georgia and South Carolina and grandfather of the present owner, Howard Morrison. A Southern agrarian, Lane introduced technologies that transformed raw natural resources into manufactured products. At Lebanon, he grew carrots that were processed and transported by rail to the Campbell Soup Company, raised dairy cows that were purchased from Mr. Carnation, and grew Satsuma oranges that were shipped to market by way of the Seaboard Railroad, on the board of which Lane served.

Despite these practical aspects of Lebanon Plantation's history, Howard Morrison's childhood memories focus

Breezes from the nearby Little Ogeechee River waft through this sleeping porch where simple furniture of wicker and iron and African-American quilts create a relaxed retreat.

instead upon its romantic role as a summertime retreat for him and his grandparents. While his father and mother stayed in town, Morrison and his siblings spent each summer at the rustic country estate where his grandmother's traditional ways still shaped the daily rhythms and rituals of life. "We slept on the porches and had a maid who lived upstairs," he reminisces. "There was an overseer with a mule named Ida and a chicken coop that produced eggs and chickens for frying. Our standard fare was rice, okra gumbo, terrapin soup, and shrimp and crab. My job was to find the *fruits de mer*. My grandmother had a great eye for mushrooms and after a rain she'd gather them and we'd have cream of mushroom soup. The butler served dinner on the porch and my grandmother would tell stories about what life was like in the old days."

Today Howard and his wife Mary, a native of Atlanta, do their best to recapture the simple pleasures of those days and to provide an old fashioned retreat for the next generation. However, the couple has significantly improved the house and added many comforts and conveniences that were previously missing. In their most significant change to the house, they converted the first-floor porch into an enclosed room that wraps around the house and provides near panoramic views of the riverside property. This room, with its seagrass rugs and painted wicker furniture, provides a decidedly informal area for relaxing and entertaining. Within the house, the entertaining rooms take on a more refined air, decorated with antiques passed down through both sides of the family, fine silver and crystal, and old paintings and prints. Yet the mood of these rooms never crosses over into a starched formality that would seem out of place in the country.

"We tried to bring the outdoors in," said Mary Reynolds Morrison, describing her collaboration with family friend and interior designer, Michael Collins. In the dining room, natural shades of green and brown relieve the formality of the antiques, which include a sideboard ornamented with lion's head drawer pulls and lion's paw feet made by an early-19th-century New York cabinet maker. Flower blossoms ornament the reproduction wallpaper and old fashioned-rug, and bird and flower prints by Catesby, Audubon, and Gould decorate the walls. "We didn't use any silk in the house," Morrison explains, "only cotton and linen. Even though some of the rooms are a little formal, it is an understated elegance." In keeping with this aesthetic, the windows in the dining room are shaded with simple shutters instead of complicated curtains and swags.

In a letter written to Collins decades before the interior designer began his work at Lebanon, Howard Morrison's grandmother voiced a prescient hope that he would some day ply his skills there. "It's just a home-a comfortable place with no pretensions-but it would welcome you with open arms," she wrote. Certainly, the bedroom that Collins designed for Howard and Mary Morrison's daughter fits this description perfectly. Although the four-poster bed, a family antique of carved mahogany with an elaborately draped and pleated canopy, is undeniably elegant, the shuttered windows, plain striped armchair, and flower-strewn needlepoint rug tip the scale toward a country informality. But nowhere is the house's relaxed bucolic air more evident than upon the screened sleeping porch. Throughout the temperate months the Morrisons sleep on the porch, bathed in the moonlight that peeks through the oaks and awakened in the morning by birdsong. A simple iron bedstead draped with colorful quilts crafted by African-Americans and an old wicker chaise longue are the only furniture in this spare plein air bedroom.

Beyond the screen door, a long porch gracefully accented by paired white columns provides the perfect spot to enjoy the breezes that come off the river. Hammocks and rocking chairs sway gently, offering the Morrisons and their guests a place to while away long afternoons and twilight hours. "We just served juleps out there last night," Mary Morrison muses, making clear that some traditions never go out of style, no matter how much the vicissitudes of time, history, and commerce may change the world at large.

Early-19th-century furniture passed down from the resident's grandmother lends an old-fashioned air of comfort combined with formality to this inviting bedroom.

Song to Summer

Yellow Cottage
Home of Michael and Erin DeLoach

Like many Savannahians, the DeLoach family has been summering on Tybee Island for generations. Although the barrier island lies a scant 20 miles due east of downtown Savannah, its breezy shores offer a welcome contrast to the city's narrow streets and squares in the summer months when the air upriver grows muggy and hot. Located at the mouth of the Savannah River, Tybee Island was a much sought after territory during the colonial period, claimed first by Spanish explorers, then in 1733, by English settlers who shared the land with Native Americans. A year-round beauty spot, the island was described by James Oglethorpe as "very agreeable" in 1733 and more poetically by John Wesley in 1736 as a place where "groves of pines running along the shore made an agreeable prospect, showing…the bloom of spring in the depth of winter." To Georgia's early settlers, however, the island's purpose was more practical than poetic, serving as the site for a lighthouse completed in 1736 that directed maritime traffic safely into the channels of the Savannah River. Three more lighthouses were built near the same site, each replacing the last as encroaching seas, violent storms, warfare, and earthquake wreaked damage on the structures.

Pleasure traffic to the island began in the mid-19th century when steamers brought visitors to its shores, but the island's heyday as a summer resort peaked in the late 19th and early 20th century when the Tybee Railroad Company linked the island to the mainland. The only one of Georgia's barrier islands accessible by public transportation for several decades, Tybee became a popular destination throughout the state and beyond. Grand hotels were constructed along its eastern shore and large private homes, modest bungalows, and pared down boarding houses multiplied, providing summer visitors a wide range of accommodations to meet their tastes and budgets. While the Victorian hotels that once lined Tybee's oceanfront are gone,

The wide-hipped roof and overhanging porches of this beach house
minimize the effects of the sun while capturing the sea breezes.

lost to fire, storm, and demolition, many of the private homes of the late 19th and early 20th century remain. But these structures are now threatened also, as modern homes, motels, and condominiums begin to crowd the beach in evidence of revived interest in the barrier island resort.

Yellow Cottage, the summer home of Michael and Erin DeLoach and their daughter, Collin, is one of the old survivors, a simple house constructed in 1915 across the street from the round-house of the Tybee Railroad Company. This typical Tybee cottage with a wide, low-pitched roof and wrap-around porches may have been used as a boarding house in the early 20th century and still serves as a rental home to summer vacationers when its owners are not in residence. "For me, buying this house was a very nostalgic thing," Michael explains. "I spent every summer on Tybee as a kid and I had a certain idea of what a Tybee house should look like, which is very un-done." Though Michael decorated the rooms of Yellow Cottage in less than a year, the results are so low-key, relaxed, and intimate that the rooms look as if they have simply evolved over decades of family living.

An interior designer who studied architecture and design at the Pratt Institute in New York, Michael describes this "undone" look as a style that is as authentic to Savannahians as their better known formal aesthetic. "Traditional Savannahians were more concerned about decorating the parlors and dining rooms of their town houses," he generalizes, explaining that their upper floors and the summer houses were often much more minimal and informal. While there is a definite minimalism to the architecture of Yellow Cottage, with its simple yellow clapboard exterior and interior surfaces of beaded board, there is evidence throughout the house of a collector's passion for bric-a-brac and a decorator's eye for detail.

Michael proudly admits to coming from a long line of collectors and art lovers including grandmothers and great-grandmothers whose possessions are scattered throughout the house and parents who are interior designers and antiques dealers. Operating DeLoach Antiques shop in downtown Savannah and DeLoach Design and Decoration with offices in New York, Charlottesville, and Savannah, Michael shares his interest in design with his wife, an art director at the prominent advertising firm, Young and Rubican. While working hard to translate his clients' tastes and visions into three-dimensions when on the job,

above: Antique wicker and bamboo furniture complement the casual, airy feel of the cottage's great room.

left: A late-19th-century, English bamboo shelf displays a collection of turquoise-glazed pottery, circa 1940.

A cabinet originally used for storing meal and grain and preparing baked goods, known as a Hoosier, serves as an impromptu bar during casual entertainments on the screened porch.

Michael enjoyed being his own client when he decorated Yellow Cottage, fulfilling his dream of the perfect island home. The cottage, with its informal, old-fashioned air, provides a pleasing contrast to the DeLoach's sleekly modern apartment in New York.

Michael's first move was to restore the house as much as possible to its original condition, removing five layers of linoleum and carpet to expose original wood flooring which he painted white to reflect the light. He tore out sheet rock that had been installed in order to reveal the original bead board and replaced areas of heart-pine paneling that had been removed over the years. Then he painted the walls in a soft palette that invoked the shades of sea and beach-pale blues and greens, sandy yellows, and sparkling whites. Inheriting a portion of his paternal grandmother's possessions soon after he bought the house, Michael decorated it partially in homage to her. "I saw this place as a combination of grandmother's house and fisherman's cottage," he says, adding that his grandmother enjoyed fishing, so the two vying fantasies mixed well.

There are three large, hospitable living spaces on the first floor-a cozy eat-in kitchen, a coolly restful great room decorated in shades of aqua, and white and an expansive screen porch that serves as both outdoor living and dining room. In the kitchen, a long table made of salvaged heart pine and an equally elongated antique bench from a British railway station creates an informal dining area. A fading sign depicting a giant loaf of bread and advertising a local grocery store mounted to one wall adds a quirky touch. Objects collected by Michael's grandmother are found throughout the room, including an old pie safe she restored with his help and emerald green stemware. A large crab pot coated with green enamel and a collection of pitchers decorated with anchors and ships provide appropriately maritime references around the room.

The marine motif finds even more direct expression in the great room, where a five-foot sailfish hangs upon the wall, leaping over a pale blue and white map depicting Tybee Island. "That's a $14.95 map in a fifty dollar frame," Michael quips, adding "this is one of the ways I like to decorate, putting a fifty-cent thing next to a five-hundred dollar piece." Old white wicker chairs that look as if they've offered generations of beach-goers a place to "sit a spell" cluster around the room. Antique wooden, bamboo, and leather furnishings add warm brown notes, balancing

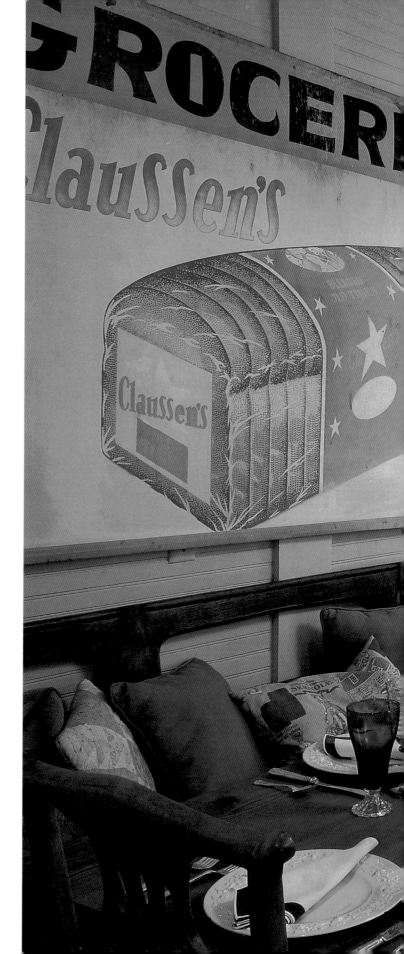

the cool shades that provide a welcome relief from the bright sun without.

From this room several windows and a door offer views onto the porch-a screened retreat offering access to the breezes that sweep the shore while keeping out the direct sun and swarming sand gnats. Here colorful accents abound, creating a festive atmosphere. Tiki lights in bright red, yellow, and green hang from the exposed rafters of the ceiling, which is painted pale blue. A delightful hodgepodge of family hand-me-downs, cherished gifts, and collector's finds establish a relaxed mood in this most casual of indoor-outdoor rooms. Mismatched chairs painted white provide seating around a table draped in a cloth woven with green and white checks. A galvanized tin watering can bursting with pear blossoms perches on a metal pedestal that Michael's grandmother found in the 1940s, an object that had previously served as an oil can display at a filling station. A green bench sitting against the yellow clapboard walls was made for this same grandmother when she was seven by a doting great-uncle. A tiny rocking chair was a gift from Michael's sister to his daughter Collin. The DeLoaches often eat supper out here in the summer, enjoying the breezes that waft across the narrow strip of land bordered by the ocean on one side and the Back River on the other.

The second floor seems to hold many more rooms than possible, with five bedrooms, two baths, and a tiny sitting room, each decorated in a distinctly different manner. The first bedroom that meets the eye has two entrances—one opening from the steep stairs that rise up the back of the house and the other, leading to the narrow hall that bisects the second floor. A giant screen painted with a Venetian ship, canvas sails aloft, rises over a massive Colonial plantation bed with six-inch diameter bed posts tinted a faded shade of haint blue-a color reputed to ward

off evil spirits. Oversized cotton buds swirl in concentric circles on the chenille bedspread, while the lines of narrow bead board paneling criss-cross the ceilings and walls. Pillows in mismatched plaids and patchwork squares add yet another level of whimsy and texture.

Just down the hall, another door opens into a sweetly serene bedroom—a meditation in blue and white that whispers promises of sleep. A delicately curved iron bedframe swathed in netting shares the floor with a white wicker rocker and an antique wicker trunk. The curtains of softly faded blue toile depicting ships at sea came from an estate sale. Michael added strips of matching blue and ivory ticking to make the old draperies fit the cottage windows. Deftly mingling tones and patterns, he chose a quilt sprigged with china blue flowers and leaves, striped sheets, and a windowpane plaid pillow for the chair.

Of all five bedrooms on the second floor, the sleeping porch that lies around the corner of the house is perhaps the greatest surprise of all. Where a wandering visitor might expect to find nothing more than a rocking chair or two tucked beneath the wide hipped roof, an entire bed-sitting room awaits, bedecked in Fourth of July finery, including a large American flag and a red glass Liberty Bell transformed into a lamp. White furniture of wicker, painted iron, and wood contrast with blue notes provided by enamelware, printed upholstery, and a brightly patterned chenille bedspread (Michael and Erin have a whole closet full of spreads that they mix and match throughout the rooms). While the sun warms this room during waking hours, at night the constant currents of seaborne air keep sleepers cool and refreshed.

Like a composer writing a tone poem, Michael has identified the essential strains of summer at the beach-sand and ships and sea, patriotic celebration, and private rest and recreation-and interwoven them into pleasing harmonies. Throughout the house, he has established and repeated leitmotifs of color, texture, and shape while constantly introducing new, surprising elements that enliven and enrich the whole. The end result is a three-dimensional song to summer that is as bold and bright and soft and sweet as the season it salutes.

A chunky plantation-made bed becomes a ship of dreams when paired with a screen painted with a stormy maritime scene.

With its red, white and blue palette, this sleeping porch is a year-round celebration of Independence Da

Collective Southern Unconscious

The Hutchins House
Home of Nancy and Richard Middleton

With its pale clapboard walls, shady porch supported by a double layer of white columns, and exuberant garden blooming with camellias, azaleas, gardenias, and magnolias, Nancy and Richard Middleton's house is a quintessential Southern dwelling. With all the characteristic details of the vernacular architecture in place, the house appears as if it might have sprung fully formed like Venus from the brow of the collective Southern unconscious. But in reality, the building is an assemblage of elements that have been slowly grafted onto a mid-19th-century structure over a period of almost 150 years. The remarkable unity of these elements and their compatibility with the Greek Revival flavor of the surrounding neighborhood testifies to the abiding quality of regional style that has permeated Southern domestic architecture throughout the centuries.

"Magnolias, porches with white columns, and dark green trim—these things call out to me," confesses Nancy Middleton, who purchased the Gordon Street house in 1994. Conjuring up a deeply implanted memory from her childhood in Memphis, Tennessee, Nancy recalls, "there was always a magnolia blossom in a bowl in the center of the dining room table." Her husband, Richard, also comes by his traditional Southern taste quite naturally, having grown up at Birdwood, a gracious Virginia country home designed by Thomas Jefferson. "We raised game birds and had hunting dogs," he recollects, "and my grandmother travelled extensively, collecting antiques and paintings."

Much like the rural English estates upon which they were modeled, Southern country seats combined the elegant with the bucolic in a graceful mélange that eventually found expression in town homes as well. Certainly the Middleton home, though distinctly urban in its proximity to the street and neighboring dwellings, maintains its country ties within, where wildlife art and an extensive collection of dog paintings, not to mention a

With its dark green wicker furniture and white columns, this porch is the quintessential Southern sanctuary.

The Middletons's house overlooks the Gothic style Wesley Monumental Methodist Church.

veritable menagerie of live dogs, cats, and birds, abound.

The house was built in 1867 and sold to a Mr. Hutchins one year later. A raised two-story frame structure, it stood well back from the street with a wide perimeter of yard separating it from its neighbors. Within the next few decades, however, the neighborhood filled up with buildings including the Wesley Monumental Methodist Church across the street, a truly monumental Gothic style building dedicated to the memory of John and Charles Wesley, and a house next door, which blocked the view from the Hutchins house of nearby Calhoun Square. Not to be outdone, the residents of the Hutchins house built an addition in 1898, adding new rooms to each of the two floors and extending the entrance hall forward an additional twenty feet. In order to bring even more light into the now shady house, this new entrance featured a glass vestibule that welcomed the suns rays without admitting the dust and noise of the street, which now passed directly below the front door.

The next major changes to the house occurred in the early to mid 20th century during the residence of the Gordon Grant family, who added small side porches and designed a garden on the western side of the property complete with a geometric parterre outlined in stone. When the Middletons acquired the house in the mid 1990s, they extended the porches, creating a double piazza running the length of the house. Reminiscent of the single-house style found frequently in Savannah and ubiquitously in nearby Charleston, this addition pays unintentional homage to Richard's ancestral connections to South Carolina's prominent Middleton family.

The Middletons also redesigned the doorways connecting the original facade of the house to the rooms created by the late-19th-century addition—replacing awkwardly narrow apertures with graceful Italianate arches

Giant house plants and animal forms—tortoise shell, pheasant feathers, and wooden deer—offset the formality of this antiques-filled dining room.

designed by Savannah architect, Dan Snyder. Local decorative painter Kip Collins was engaged to decorate the interior walls with images and surfaces that evoke the Greek and Italian roots of Southern Classical Revival styles. In the hallway Collins painted a pair of Corinthian columns on either side of the arched entrance to the stair hall and in the dining room he covered the wall in paints and glazes that translated Nancy's request for walls resembling the timeworn surfaces of Tuscan farm houses into glowing reality.

Like the exterior of the house, the entertaining rooms artfully combine an array of objects which, taken together, express the essential elements of Southern style. Faded velvet and hand-worked needlepoint upholstery cover antique furniture of European and American provenance-some of which are cherished hand-me-downs, including a pair of chairs that graced Birdwood's parlor in Richard's grandmother's time. Exotic Asian objects, including a 19th century Japan chest and an 18th century red lacquer Chinese wedding chest, point to the Southern penchant for oriental design—an inclination they inherited from their European forebears and trading partners. A portrait of a Baltimore lady by renowned 19th-century portraitist Thomas Sully, a hunting scene by French artist Eugene Petite, and oil and watercolor impressions of Moroccan life reflect the traditional spectrum of Southern taste in art. New curtains in a crisply tailored plaid provide the only contemporary note in the room and serve to suggest that elegant design is not limited to the past.

Against the burnished walls of the dining room, more artwork represents additional interests shared by Southern connoisseurs. A large Native American scene painted by an artist from the Taos School and purchased by Richard's great-grandmother dominates one wall. Across the room, an arrangement of five paintings by 19th-century Scottish and American artists depict dogs of various sizes and breeds. A fascination with wildlife runs throughout the room where pheasant feathers fan out before a fireplace flanked by wooden deer carved in China and lit by the amber glow of a lamp fashioned from a tortoise shell. Although Richard breaks the Southern mold by preferring not to hunt, he does enjoy collecting images of animals. A rare portfolio of bird prints by Martinét are mounted along the stair hall and more dog and wildlife scenes ornament his second-floor study.

While the dining room table and chairs are new reproductions of traditional designs, the sideboards are antique. One dating from the mid 19th century came from a home in Macon, Georgia. The other, a massive Empire piece carved of solid mahogany, has been in Richard's family for generations. This heirloom, along with the mirror over the mantel, a central Virginia piece dating from the 1820s and reputedly made by gypsies, and the crystal chandelier, all hale from Birdwood. In a final nod to the post-war collecting habits of the South, a scene of a Civil War engagement between two iron-clad ships painted by 19th-century Savannah artist and organist Augustus Gustin hangs in the corner of the dining room.

Although the piazza extending along the western side of the Middleton's house has been recently redesigned, it has a timeless air contributed in part by the use of traditional shapes and materials. Ample wicker furniture, jardinieres overflowing with geraniums and ferns, and gently whirring ceiling fans all proffer the kind of hospitality for which southern porches are famous. Nancy recently came out one afternoon to enjoy the prospect of her garden in the sun's warm glow and fell asleep in one of the wicker chairs. "It's wonderful to sit on the porch and look over the garden," she explains, without discriminating between the vision of the waking eye or that of the enchanted sleeper. But enchantment definitely plays a role in the garden that lies below the porch's rail.

At first glance, the landscape below seems to be traditional and formal, with its herringbone brick paths, raised beds planted with bright annuals, and cast iron fountain burbling in its center. But a secret garden lies at the back of the yard, hidden beyond a wooden pergola overgrown with vines. Through this dark tunnel, glimpses of another world unfold: an aqueous paradise where the graceful calligraphy of palm fronds and bamboo reflect in the still water of a lily-pond that offers a retreat for carp and thirsty birds.

"I bought the house because of that garden," exclaims Nancy. "It looks like something from a story book about an enchanted land." And though she refers specifically to her secret garden, she might be describing her home as well and the entire Southern vernacular architecture to which it belongs. These buildings, with their shared language of signs and symbols, also belong to an enchanted land that dwells somewhere between the poles of fact and fantasy. They are the physical remains of the American South, a place of complex truths that lies buried deep beneath the tangled overgrowth of history and memory.

Palazzo Style

The Hammond House
Ben Adams' Pied-a-Terre

above: The prim facade of this house belies its interior, which includes a quirky antiques store and an even more eccentric pied-a-terre.

right: Each surface in the pied-a-terre is decorated with a curious array of objects. This militaristic tableau is crowned with an ornate Italian urn dating from the mid-19th century.

On the twelfth night of January each year, Ben Adams hosts a Canterbury Tales party. Eight to ten close friends are in attendance: the men in tails, the women, jewels. They gather in a century-old dining room ornamented with plaster nymphs, porcelain birds, and a marble and alabaster urn that once adorned a funeral home. Before the eight-course meal begins, guests draw numbers determining the order of the ensuing events. As dinner progresses, the numbers are called and each guest performs an original poem, song, or story. "At first, some were self-conscious," Adams confides, "but now, people beg to be invited and I have to limit the number to ten because they are apt to wax eloquent."

The only silent presence in the room is the portrait of a miser, which Adams purchased from Jim Williams, Savannah antiques dealer and protagonist of *Midnight in the Garden of Good and Evil.* "That painting hung in Jim's study the night of the shooting," Adams intones dramatically. "If only it could speak, the stories it would tell!" Fortunately, Adams speaks freely and with great relish, telling the tales of the many beloved possessions that grace his home. He begins an account of the house's previous owners, three in total including Nina Pape, co-founder of the Girl Scouts of America, and Miss Pape's niece, Florence Crane Schwalb, who shared the honor of being the first Girl Scout with co-founder Juliette Gordon Low's niece, Daisy Lawrence.

The house was constructed in 1879 for Mary Hammond, who lived there alone for many years before it passed into the hands of Miss Pape and her neice. During the 1970s, Adams ran an antiques shop a few buildings down Gwinnett Street from the house, and frequently chatted with Mrs. Schwalb as she completed her daily constitutional. One day, she confided in him that she was going to have to paint her home—a large frame house with Italianate and Queen Anne detail—and that the cost was going to ruin her. A consummate gentleman and

businessman as well, Adams offered to buy the house over time, permitting her to remain there until her death—and within days, the deal was sealed. As tenants gradually vacated the house's ground-floor apartments, Adams moved in, room by room. He completed the move after Mrs. Schwalb's death, relocating his antiques shop, Antiques Alley, to the first two floors and creating an eccentric pied-a-terre above (Adams lives in a nearby suburb with his wife, Betty).

"I had all these things I didn't want to sell," he explains, "so I decided to decorate two rooms with them. I created a bed/sitting room, then another room, and then a kitchen. Before I knew it, I had a whole play house," he exclaims gleefully. Indeed, the pied-a-terre does have the fanciful air of a place created more for whimsy than for work-a-day life. All the walls are painted a chocolatey shade of pink-a deeply blushing beige dubbed Monk Brown. A large copy of a Guido Reni painting in a style Adams calls "Chocolate Box Art" ornaments one wall of the third-floor drawing room. Adams claims to have purchased a box of Whitman's candies with the same painting on its top for his mother decades ago. The original hangs in a palazzo in Rome.

When asked to give a name to his own decorative style, Adams flirted briefly with *bordello baroque* before settling at last on *palazzo style*. He is the first to admit that his style is a little bit over the top. "I don't mind if people say my house is tacky," he demurs. "But for goodness sake, just don't let them call it dull!" On a more serious note, Adams, a native Texan, explains that his décor fits within the bounds of what he considers to be true Savannah style.

"This is a late-19th-century house with some Victorian things in it, a lot of hand-me-downs, and pieces I've collected because I like them," he explains. Authentic Savannah homes-those that haven't been done over in one particular style or another-display this same eclecticism. "Most of the houses lived in by Savannahians mix up a

range of different styles because they weren't decorated within a single generation," Adams adds.

Adams himself decorates largely according to whim. The unlikely mélange of furnishings and decorative objects in his ultra-posh bedroom best exemplifies the result of this highly personal approach to design. An English bed, circa 1880, is fashioned of bleached pine in the French style and surmounted by an Italianate gilt cornice board hung with a fringed pelmet. Adams suspects that the side tables, though originally thought to be English, are in fact Venetian. The desk is reproduction Louis XV; the rug, a Chinese import; and the chandelier, Adams says, can only be described as "Early 1970s." The total effect falls somewhere in between the boudoir of a jaded Venetian voluptuary and a set for a 1920s period romance starring Lillian Gish or Rudolph Valentino.

Perhaps the most delightful thing about this room is the stories each object tells, with Adam's deft assistance. "I found the slippers in an antiques fair in Brighton," Adams recounts, referring to a pair of gilt-embroidered Venetian mules near the bed. "There were two impeccably dressed Englishmen at the stall and when they asked 22 pounds for the slippers, I demanded to know what on earth convinced them to pay so much in the first place that they had to charge me such a price. They confessed to being as drunk as lords at the time." When Adams complained of being stone cold sober, the Englishmen proceeded to mix him gin-and-tonics on the spot, lower the price, and sweeten the deal with the promise of brunch until, at last, he caved in and cried, "Wrap the slippers!"

Not surprisingly, the gilded, blackamoor figure in the drawing room has a similarly colorful provenance. "It's probably mid-19th-century Italian," Adams estimates. "I acquired it years ago from friends in Brighton—I used to sit in a chair next to him during their open-house parties. It

This eclectic bedroom clearly expresses the resident's "more is better" philosophy of decor.

took me five years to talk them into selling it to me." Plaster casts of the Marquis de Lafayette and John Paul Jones share the room, which is furnished with an 1880s suite of armchairs and sofa upholstered in Aubusson tapestries. Books and bibelots ornament every surface in a more-is-better philosophy of decorating. "Nature abhors a vacuum, and I'm doing my part to help out," Adams quips.

The apartment is full of tableaux that seem devised to encourage guests to stop and demand an explanation. A guest room blooms with plumed hats, beaded handbags, and outré sunglasses that once belonged to a Savannah socialite. A hall table supports a militaristic display including a signed photograph of Kaiser Wilhelm, a collection of ivory miniatures depicting King George IV and his admirals, a United States Naval Academy sword, and a helmet from the Royal Canadian mounted police. In the card room, a felt-topped table is perpetually set for bridge and sherry. While nearly all the furniture in this last room was inherited from Adams's mother-in-law (he couldn't bear to sell the heirlooms, so he decorated a room with them as a Christmas present to his wife), a table top is scattered with old photographs of complete strangers. A visitor once exclaimed, "How lovely to have all those family pictures—who are all those people?" "I haven't the slightest idea," Adams replied. "But I could make up a story about every single one."

A piece of circa-1900-Italian garden statuary graces the hallway.

Ardsley Park Eclectic

The Trosdal House
Home of Dr. and Mrs. Jules Victor, III

The pastel stucco facade of this Ardsley Park house reveals the early 20th century penchant for Mediterranean Revival.

The approach to Barbara and Bubba Victor's house is unmistakably Spanish in effect. Entering from Abercorn Street, an oak-lined avenue of Ardsley Park, guests must pass through an iron gate and tower-like portal to reach the cool shade of a pink stucco porch. Heavy wooden shutters, terra cotta amphora, and curling brackets of wrought iron complete the Iberian mood. Overwhelmed by the massive scale of this front entrance, most guests prefer to let themselves in through the gate in the garden wall. Along the exterior of this wall, bristling plantings of Spanish bayonets and twisting ironwork reinforce the Mediterranean flavor of the house. Flowering vines dangle over the top of this weathered stucco expanse, offering tantalizing hints of the beauty that lies beyond.

On the far side of the gate, a large garden unfolds in several room-like spaces, which seamlessly unite a far-flung range of influences: Spanish austerity, French formality, Asian exoticism, and pure Savannah style. An oval pond

In the hallway an antique Italian console table is flanked by French chairs and surmounted by a Venetian mirror and Catesby bird prints.

planted with waterlilies and papyrus forms the centerpiece of the garden. In its midst, a bronze fountain gently cascades. Along the perimeter of this rectangular garden, azaleas and camellias, though Asian in origin, lend a distinctively Southern air. At the far end of the garden, the sinuous lines of wrought iron gates repeat the Spanish motif, while square parterres filled with white gravel and flowering plants create a French impression.

Although the geometric lines of the garden tend toward the formal, the abundant plantings and intimate scale of the walled enclosure creates a relaxing, hospitable environment. Indeed, the adjoining terrace, equipped with an outdoor kitchen and furnished with several circular tables, is Barbara and Bubba's favorite place to entertain. "This is our summer kitchen," says Barbara. "We love eating outdoors and enjoying the garden in all the different seasons." But when extreme heat or winter's chill drives the Victors indoors, they still appreciate the gardens that wrap around two sides of the house from within. "I wanted the whole emphasis of the house to focus on bringing the garden inside," Barbara explains. To do this, the Victors enclosed the long side porch extending along the one side of the house to create a sun room overlooking Abercorn Street and the garden.

In the formal living room, Barbara introduced tones of azalea pink, grass green, and sun-warmed terra cotta in newly upholstered furnishings. Keeping the original Chinese chintz curtains that were hanging in the room when they bought the house seven years ago, Barbara added a Japanese screen emblazoned with birds and flowers that echo the natural world beyond the room's tall windows. Asian ceramics and Oriental rugs add more color and pattern, while a dark bronze sculpture of an American Indian reclining upon a heavily carved Gothic style table introduces a full complement of eclectic influences to the

Another salvaged mantel provides a dark note in the warmly glowing dining room.

room's interior. The architectural setting demonstrates an equally wide stylistic spectrum, combining the Spanish-inspired open-beam ceiling hung with iron chandeliers with the classical black marble mantle salvaged from a mansion designed by Regency architect William Jay.

This unlikely aesthetic juxtaposition is characteristic of the free-wheeling revivalism that reigned in American architecture during the 1910s and 20s when automobile suburbs such as Ardsley Park and the adjacent Chatham Crescent were being developed. Architectural historian Roulhac Toledano characterizes the area's architecture as "running the gamut of revival and eclectic styles . . . [with] Spanish castles, Greek-provenance mansions, Italian villas, and even Louisiana plantation houses."[1] One of the first two houses to be built in Ardsley Park, the Victors' home was designed for the Trosdal family by one of Savannah's most popular and skilled architects, Hyman Witcover, first president of the Savannah Society of Architects and designer of both City Hall and the Public Library main branch on Bull Street.

In order to entice people to move out to the new suburbs, notable architects like Witcover were hired by the area's developers to build homes combining the best elements of Savannah's downtown mansions—elegant appointments and classically inspired details—with all the advantages of the suburbs, including modern floor plans within and spacious gardens without. The end result of these homes, with their grand scale, nostalgic anachronisms, and early-20th-century luxuries, invokes the glamour of early Hollywood film sets. The attractions of the Trosdal home were not lost on Barbara, who grew up surrounded with Mediterranean style architecture in San Diego, and Bubba who, like many native Savannahians, spent his childhood in Ardsley Park. Both were immediately drawn to the pink stucco garden villa on Abercorn Street.

above and right: The extensive garden combines traditional Southern flora with French parterres and Spanish wrought-iron elements.

Described by its previous owner as "everyone's favorite Ardsley Park house," the home had been carefully protected over the years. Only three families lived in it prior to the Victors and each left the original decorative details in place: the crystal chandelier in the dining room, the ornate fireplaces (including a wooden mantel in the dining room carved with a scene of medieval revelry), delicate parquet flooring in the living room, and a bold checkerboard pattern of black and white marble in the hall. Each of the former residents also contributed to the house's appearance, one laying out the formal gardens in the rear, and another inviting Georgia architect and interior designer, Frank McCall, to reconfigure the living room, originally divided into two rooms, into a single cavernous entertaining space.

In keeping with this tradition, the Victors have largely preserved the house as they found it, cherishing its complex bouquet of styles and tastes. Barbara kept the gold foil wallpaper that lends a lustrous glow to the walls of the dining room, as well as the valances covered in patterned silk that crown its windows. She ordered matching silk to create draperies and painted the ceiling a deep shade of strawberry to compliment the curtains. In the living room, Barbara added warm highlights of gold leaf and terra cotta paint to the ceiling's beams and brackets. And in the hall, she painted and glazed the walls a deep shade of sunflower yellow.

In the garden behind the house, the Victors have also left their mark, extending the stone terrace along the rear facade and installing their plein-air kitchen. Barbara regularly adds new plantings that enhance the existing garden plan without obscuring it. "We love this house," Barbara exclaims as she gazes over her domain. And the house, with all its burnished charm, clearly basks in this regard.

The Cohen House
Home of Park and Aline Callahan

above: Whimsical arrangements of cherished objects, including these ivory netsuke, play games with scale.

right: Even though it received Second Empire baroque embellishments in the late nineteenth century, the facade of this Greek Revival house still demonstrates mid-century restraint.

The Greek Revival style can range in mood from the flamboyant to the severe. While the high style is often expressed by a busy layering of classically inspired elements, the more restrained end of the spectrum tends towards elegant geometries and minimal embellishment. This latter description best suits the Cohen House, a wood frame structure built on a raised basement in 1852 by Jacob and Isaac Cohen and their sister Elizabeth, prominent members of Savannah's thriving Jewish community. Located on West Jones Street in Pulaski Ward, the house originally boasted little external decoration except a columned portico, which was more practical than ornamental in intent.

Even though the house was remodeled and enlarged in 1872 in the Second Empire baroque style by John Lynch Martin, a cotton grower and factor who added bracketed cornices, a mansard roof, and dormer windows, the exterior still maintains a reserved appearance. Within, the house's entertaining rooms echo the elegant minimalism of its composed gray and white facade. Three adjoining rectangles with heart-pine floors and high ceilings, these rooms are sparely ornamented with simple Greek Revival door and window surrounds and stately marble mantels. This simplicity was one of the chief charms the building held for Park and Aline Callahan, who purchased it in 1978 when they were seeking a house for themselves and their collection of antique and modern furniture and art.

A native Georgian and an architect with degrees from Princeton and Georgia Tech, Park has done considerable preservation work in Savannah over the years. Yet despite his familiarity with traditional homes and a Southern upbringing surrounded by European and American antiques, his over-riding aesthetic is unquestionably modern. Signature furniture designed by modernist gurus anchor the first-floor rooms, including Barcelona chairs and a glass-topped coffee table created by Mies van der Rohe

Elegant geometries unite modernist furniture of glass and steel with English and American antiques and a Renaissance Revival mantel of the living room.

The X-shaped legs of a Barcelona chair are echoed by the silhouette of an antique butler's table and the hour-glass form depicted in a 20th century print hanging over the mantel.

for the Barcelona pavilion, and a large Parsons table in the dining room. In a spirit of bold eclecticism, this table is surrounded by a suite of Italian reproduction Chinese Chippendale chairs upholstered in a 1960s zebra print.

"Eclecticism is the best word to describe our style," explains Aline. A Frenchwoman who grew up in Morocco's royal capital of Rabat (her father was personal physician to the king) and finally settled in the American South, Aline comes by her eclectic style quite naturally. "You should never be afraid to mix the old with the new, to blend objects of value with things of no value, as long as you keep them within the right proportions and don't lose touch with the whimsical."

Unexpected yet pleasing proportions are one of the hallmarks of the Callahans's combined aesthetic. Often, Savannahians will respond to the high ceilings, tall windows, and heavy mantels of rooms like the Callahans's front parlor by using large-scale furnishings, rich colors, and lush textiles in an effort to match the architectural grandeur. But the Callahans chose to balance the room's scale by placing a low, informal sofa dressed in a crisp canvas slipcover between the nine-over-nine windows. They paired this with the minimalist chrome and glass table, and instead of using overstuffed wing chairs opted for the spare lines of Barcelona chairs. Antique butler's tables introduce a more traditional note to the room, but their simple lines complement, rather than contradict, the silhouettes of the modernist furnishings.

A plain sisal rug covers the glossy wood floor and, in lieu of heavy draperies, overgrown bird of paradise plants filter the light that pours in through the two tall windows. These massive plants tower over the room's small sofa and introduce an undeniable note of wit to the setting. The contrast in scale between the massive marble mantel and the diminutive artifacts arrayed upon it –Mycenaean and Cycladic Greek and pre-Columbian American Indian objects all less than six

inches tall-seems equally playful in intent and successful in effect. Contemporary paintings and prints reiterate the room's geometries of intersecting lines and graceful arcs while adding warm earth tones that balance its neutral palette.

Despite the disparity in age, style, and material of the decorative elements of this room, the total effect is one of unity and exquisite balance. The furnishings and decorative elements in the dining room revisit the themes established in the front parlor. The walls are painted a deep charcoal brown and the simple Greek Revival fireplace of slate has been faux-grained to resemble pale yellow marble veined with grey. The modern dining table and chairs, with their tortoise and bamboo finishes, expand upon the brown and gold color scheme. Traditional art and antiques tucked away in the corner, including a 1787 portrait by an itinerant American artist, a Hepplewhite chest, and Sheffield candlesticks, counterbalance the room's contemporary elements. Again, tiny objects adorn the mantel-a collection of ivory netsuke, stone eggs, and Chinese snuff bottles anchored around a large ostrich egg.

Beyond the dining room door lies a modern kitchen and sitting room addition designed by the Callahans. Overlooking the courtyard garden below, it is intended to resemble a 19th century porch converted into an interior room. Large windows allow Aline to survey fish ponds below where giant Japanese carp swim and a green garden, which demonstrates the same play of scale and texture that is evident throughout the house. This lush garden, surrounded by high walls and trees, reminds Aline of Morocco. While large windows frame this vista, a door opening into the dining room provides an interior view through the three entertaining rooms to the front of the house.

"I love this house," Aline remarks. "The high ceilings, the light flooding in through large windows, the way the rooms open into each other . . . these all give a sense of space and serenity. It reminds me of the beautiful extended views of Moroccan houses overlooking courtyards with fountains and lush, vibrant vegetation."

In the upstairs rooms, Aline more specifically invoked the dual design traditions of France and Morocco with which she grew up. She upholstered the walls of the master bedroom with fabric woven by the House of Braquenié, a textile manufacturing firm founded in Paris in 1823. While the custom of covering walls with padded cloth is French, the Persian pattern Aline chose invites comparison to the complex motifs of Moroccan ceramics and textiles. For furniture, she chose a selection of antiques from the reign of Louis XVI, which reinforces the décor's French feel.

While the wide-ranging influences expressed in their décor significantly expand the traditional vocabulary of Savannahian eclecticism, the Callahans's aesthetic is, in fact, quite in keeping with their adopted city's tastes. Many Savannah homes in the 19th century blended European and American furnishings spanning a century or more of design with exotic objects reflecting the worldly trade of a port city and former English colony. Souvenirs from travel and Asian decorative objects were often displayed upon classically inspired mantelpieces in centuries past. And contemporary art and furnishings always found a place in the well-appointed Savannah home. The ease with which the Callahans's diverse collection of antique and modern objects blends with the architecture of this mid-19th-century house reveals the basic truth behind eclecticism: good design has the power to transcend artificial boundaries of place, time, and style.

Great Circle

Conrad Aiken's Childhood Home
Home of Furlow Gatewood and John Rosselli

above: The wide triple sash windows of this mid-19th-century house are just one of several attractions that drew John Rosselli and Furlow Gatewood to this house.

right: The unapologetically faux marble paintwork that reveals rather than conceals the wide wooden floorboards of the hall offsets the room's otherwise formal character.

The historic marker set before Conrad Aiken's childhood home refers obliquely to the violent crime that occurred behind the placid brick facade it indicates. The bronze letters spell out the wheres and whens of Aiken's life. A renowned man of letters, he lived in this house until his parent's tragic death in 1901, after which he moved to New England and went on to attend Harvard, win the Pulitzer Prize in 1930, and the National Book Award in 1954. According to the plaque, he returned to Savannah in 1962 to live next door to his childhood home. Though accurate, these hard facts do little to enlighten the stranger about the bizarrely romantic events that framed the life of Conrad Aiken: a poet who was orphaned at the age of eleven when his father murdered his mother then killed himself, and who felt compelled, sixty-one years later, to return to the scene of the crime. A careful reading of Aiken's prolific and often cryptic prose and poetry provides some insights into this peculiar gyration, particularly his novel *Great Circle*. John Berendt devotes three pages of *Midnight in the Garden of Good and Evil* to the poet's story, describing a visit to the Aiken family grave site in Bonaventure Cemetery, before declaring, "I was beguiled by Savannah."

Clearly Aiken was also beguiled by Savannah, which he described as "that most magical of cities…that earthly paradise." So, too, are the current residents of the Aiken's childhood home, who bought it after touring the city in 1988. "We were visiting and fell in love with all the houses and that was it," explains Furlow Gatewood, who shares the house with John Rosselli. Gatewood and Rosselli also share a passion for antiques, which developed into the thriving John Rosselli International, a New York-based company specializing in antiques and custom painted reproductions. At home in Savannah, this passion permeates their home, which is decorated with an

A monumental French neoclassical painting of
"Diana and the Hunt" adds a dramatic classical
element to this playfully eclectic room.

A faux-finished screen designed in the Rosselli workshops provides an
elegant backdrop for a collection of objets d'art.

This porch, designed by Furlow Gatewood, unites the studied elegance of the interior with the romantic quality of the overgrown garden behind the house.

extensive array of antique and reproduction furniture and art. Today, the house gleams under the attentive eyes and hands of its custodians, but this was not the case before their residence. Although the previous owner had lots of marvelous English and American furniture, according to Rosselli the house was in a condition of decay with peeling paint, rotting floors on the street level, and a garden obscured with weeds and debris. While in this state of decrepitude, the house may have served as a more effective medium for the tragic past that unfolded in its midst, but its recently acquired glow of style and elegance clearly celebrates the present.

"It's really meant to be a house where you can breathe and sit and be comfortable," says Rosselli, who uses it primarily as a getaway from his hectic New York life[1]. Both Gatewood and Rosselli were drawn to the house by its amply proportioned triple-sash windows which brighten the house throughout the day. French doors opening onto a screened porch at the rear of the house maximize the flow of light and air from its garden side. Gatewood's favorite room, this back porch takes full advantage of this exposure, welcoming cool breezes and overlooking a verdant garden paved with mossy bricks and centered around a cast-iron fountain. "When we bought this house, the fountain was there," Gatewood explains, "but we couldn't tell what else was out there, the garden was so overgrown with grass and weeds."

Rosselli's preferred haunt is the second-floor sitting room, which commands a view of the boulevard below and cemetery across the street. Painted a vibrant red, Rosselli's favorite shade for intimate rooms, the study is ornamented with a collection of Orientalist paintings and figures depicting camels, sun-baked ruins and dark-skinned figures adorned with flowing robes and silken turbans. Layered fabrics and pillows cover the furnishings of this room, creating a lavish lair that matches the art in exoticism. The bedroom that lies beyond, also painted red and decorated in the Orientalist mode, features an eclectic mix of furnishings including a canopied four-poster bed of carved mahogany and a screen produced by Rosselli's workshops featuring a Hindustani scene inspired by Zuber wallpaper.

The bright color scheme of this bedroom suite is the exception rather than the rule for the house, which displays far more chromatic restraint on the parlor level. This floor is accessed by a steep brick stair with cast-iron railings that

Filled with an unlikely melange of dog art and objets d'art, Orientalist paintings, and antique and modern textiles, this second floor study provides a deeply personal and satisfying retreat.

Antique Delft tiles surround a large fireplace in the original kitchen located on the ground floor of the house.

A crystal éperne piled high with fruit forms a traditional centerpiece in the small, yet opulent dining room.

ascends to a doorway surrounded by rectangular window lights. A louvered exterior door allows the residents to leave the solid inner door open in mild weather, allowing sunlight and cool breezes to penetrate the hall. Unlike most Savannah houses, which typically have narrow stairhalls running the length of one side, the Aiken House has a square entrance hall accented by a graceful stair which winds up and around its walls. Rosselli and Gatewood hired Bob Christian, a decorative painter who trained in their workshop and now lives and works in Savannah, to cover the wooden floor with a faux-marble pattern inspired by a Regency design. While the pattern flirts with Southern formality, the evident trumpery involved in the simulation reveals the owners' determination to maintain a relaxed and informal air.

The use of sisal throughout the house, including a runner on the stairs and a large rug in the living room, reinforces this casual mood. In this large double parlor, Rosselli and Gatewood mounted shutters in lieu of curtains and hung ceiling fans from the plaster medallians instead of chandeliers. This toned-down setting provides the perfect backdrop for highly ornamental elements including a pair of marbelized Corinthian columns capped by urns, Venetian mirrors, and massive neoclassical paintings of ancient architectural and mythological scenes. Contemporary chairs designed by Billy Baldwin and upholstered in Belgian linen offer the eye a place to rest amid the animal prints, floral tapestries, and stripes that cover a free-wheeling mélange of furniture. The residents' unrestrained eclecticism finds full expession in one corner of the room where a Rosselli reproduction table painted in the Chinese manner bears a collection of figurines and bibelots including Empire candlesticks in the shape of griffins, Asian pagodas, and buddhas and porcelain hippopatami carrying obelisks on their backs.

"I surround myself with anything that catches my eye," Gatewood confesses. "That's the fun of collecting—not being restricted." Rosselli, whom Gatewood accuses of not being able to go to the barber without coming home with something, is equally enthusiastic about collecting. "When you collect things and have so many things," he explains, "you have to layer them together."

This design philosophy is perhaps most evident in the dining room, a small square chamber behind the entrance hall where every surface is covered with decorative objects. The faux-marble design from the hall continues onto the floor of this room. On either side of a dark marble mantel, painted consoles designed in the Rosselli workshops support blue and white antique porcelain and crystal compotes. More porcelain hangs on the walls, along with crystal and brass wall sconces, oil paintings depicting aviary scenes, and racks of deer horns. Elaborate crystal candelabra stand on the marble mantel. A dazzling chandelier with cascading chains of pendants hangs above a Regency dining table. Upon the table sits a crystal epergne laden with fruit, which rises up to nearly meet the chandelier's bottom-most tier.

A restrained sense of playfulness pervades this room, preventing its "more is more" décor from crossing the line into oppressive formality. There is a feeling of spontaneity and whimsy here and throughout the house that effectively erases any residue of tragedy that once stained its walls. "I cannot take these things with me, and other people will own them," Rosselli philosophizes. "But I will try to take care of them as much as possible and not be precious about them." Time passes, memory fades, things and even places change hands-this is the lesson these rooms convey, a lesson Conrad Aiken clearly discovered during his voyage through life, which began and ended in this same row of homes.

Interior shutters painted Factors Walk Red, a color created by resident Ann Osteen, echo the hue of the bricks surrounding the central window.

Chromatic Essence

The Taylor Building
Home of Ann and Lamont Osteen

It is hard to know what excites Ann Osteen most about Savannah–the vibrant hues of its architectural and natural setting, the varied patterns and textures of its timeworn surfaces, or the piquant history of its boom-town days. Breathlessly describing the 19th-century Savannahians she finds so intriguing, Ann exclaims, "We had what everybody wanted: we were rich; we could buy anything we liked; we were the French of the New South. We bought beautiful things from all over the world. We were on the cutting edge of design." A woman of infectious enthusiasms and well-honed skills as an artist, colorist, and designer, she concludes, "I wanted to tell people about it."

This "telling" began with the creation of Ann's line of Savannah paint colors and textile designs that were produced and marketed by Martin Senour and Scalamandre. "It all started when I saw peeling paint on a building and picked up a wino's broken bottle and scraped the wall down to its original color," says Ann. She kept scraping buildings and studying her surroundings for several more months, identifying a selection of colors that tells the history of Savannah and its people and recreating them with her artist's paints. Well before internationally-renowned companies began promoting her work, Ann created what her friends jokingly called her "turned-on color cookies." This nickname derived from the fact that her first set of color samples was painted on balsa wood squares mounted on a cookie sheet she presented as a research project at a Junior League meeting. "Everyone snickered," she recalls, except the director of Historic Savannah Foundation, who realized that she was capturing in pigment the chromatic essence of Savannah.

Factors Walk Red, for instance, was inspired by the pressed Philadelphia bricks ships carried in their holds *en route* to Savannah in the late 18th and early 19th century. This bright red brick was the preferred facing material for

Rugged compositions of brick and ballast stone line the passageways that parallel the river's edge.

the street-side facades of commercial buildings along the Savannah River waterfront, a stretch of which came to be called Factors Walk in honor of the cotton factors who traded there. A combination of the cheaper Savannah gray bricks and ballast stones was preferred for the less ornamented riverside exposures.

There are a few lines of Philadelphia brick running through the roughly textured exterior walls of the 19th-century cotton complex Ann owns with her husband, Lamont. This structure is the oldest surviving commercial building on the Savannah River bluff. Constructed by William Taylor in 1818 as part of a larger cotton warehouse and store complex, the building stands atop a maze of tunnels that connect it with the Chart House on the corner. Today, its lower levels house a restaurant and an art gallery where Ann's paintings and design items are for sale, and its upper two floors accommodate the Osteen's loft-like home. Like most of the structures that line the river's edge, the Osteens' house is built below street level. Steep stairs and walkways lead down from Bay Street to the pedestrian promenade that runs along the riverfront and provides access to the waterside entrances of the buildings.

From the Bay Street side, the Osteens' house is approached by a narrow pedestrian bridge spanning the cobblestone canyon that slopes down to the river. This bridge leads to the front door of the home, which opens into the fourth floor of the building. The weathered texture of this wooden bridge and craggy stone walls of the house are offset by the crisp and glossy lines of a door and two window frames painted a shade Ann calls Geechee Teal-a color inspired by the neckbands of ducks that frequent the nearby Ogeechee river. Glimpses of Factors Walk Red can be seen through the windows that open into the Osteens' master bedroom-a large room painted entirely in that bright shade. An art deco brass bed forms a distinctive focal

Ann Osteen's daring artistry is evident in the master bedroom, painted Factors Walk Red and decorated with boldly shaped furniture including an art deco brass bed.

point in this room and serves as a stylistic touchstone for Ann, who found it abandoned in a South Carolina field years ago. Attracted by the bed's silhouette, she brought it home only later to discover that it is attributed to the designer who created the brass railings at Radio City Music Hall. The bed's bold cursive lines inspired a whole host of associations that informed the design choices Ann made while transforming the old cotton warehouse into a boldly modern home.

"It reminded me of the curved railings and walls of the ferries we used to take in the summer at Chesapeake Bay," explains Ann, a native of tidewater Maryland. With these ferries in mind, Ann worked with architect Juan Bertotto to create an open-plan design for the home featuring curved walls that partially enclose a series of rooms. Also inspired by the ferries she adored as a child, Ann painted the walls in with a high-gloss finish. The open-rung stair ascending to the top floor provides yet another maritime reference. Original to the structure, it was constructed by the ship chandlers who built the warehouse and not surprisingly bears a close resemblance to the wooden ladders used onboard seafaring craft.

The shiny curved walls and open plan also invite comparison to the ship-like designs of French modernist, Le Corbusier. Direct quotations of Le Corbusier can be found throughout the house, including center-pivot doors and his famous chrome and leather *chaise longue* placed in a platform-like seating area on the top floor. This area, approached by the open stair, faces a wall of windows framing views of the Savannah River and the Talmadge Bridge. A circular firepit of brick and slate sits upon the heart-pine floor and is crowned by a spoked circle of wood that hangs from the open beam ceiling. A giant cotton winch, this wheel was originally suspended vertically and used to hoist bales of cotton from one level of the warehouse to another.

The circular wooden winch that now creates a dramatic decorative element was once suspended vertically from the ceiling and used to hoist huge bales of cotton.

While the cotton winch is original to Savannah, the remaining influences in this sitting area are far-flung, ranging from French modernism to Western ski lodges (the fire pit) and Marin County Redwood homes (the open beam ceiling). Yet many of the decorative influences remain closer to home, including the wagon-wheel quilt sewn by a Georgia craftswoman that hangs over the stairs on a wall painted Tabby White, a color named for the mixture of lime, sand, and shell that was one of the Georgia colony's first building materials.

To today's eye, the loft-style modernism of this home seems quite familiar, but at the time it was designed in the 1970s, it was utterly innovative. In fact, Ann suspects that she experimented with loft-style living well before it became the rage in New York's SoHo district. Certainly, the Osteens were the first residents of Factors Walk to remodel an old warehouse in this contemporary style. When they purchased the building thirty years ago, Factors Walk was a seedy, rundown waterfront with little or no residential activity at all. Yet as an artist, Osteen felt comfortable there since the Savannah Art Association had operated a school and a gallery in the area for several years. In fact, Osteen felt more at home along the gritty, colorful waterfront than she did in her traditional Ardsley Park house where she had been living for a decade in what she calls "Georgia style," with a maid and a yardman, antiques galore, and a pageant of society tea parties given for local charities.

"My husband and I wanted to do something truly different, and we didn't want to do it in an old house and destroy it," she explains. So the Osteens bought the dilapidated waterfront property and went to work, saving what elements they could and adding new ones that gave expression to their iconoclastic sensibilities. The result is an unusual home, which, like Osteen's colors, celebrates the essence of Savannah in new and surprising ways.

By leaving many of the rugged, utilitarian elements of the warehouse's structure in place-its wide floor boards, ship's ladder stair, and cotton winch-the Osteens pay homage to King Cotton, the ruling monarch of the city's export economy for more than a century. By integrating decidedly contemporary design elements, the couple follows in the footsteps of well-to-do Savannahians of the late 18th and 19th centuries who made every effort to adopt the most *au courant* styles and design trends in their homes. By acting as urban pioneers, repopulating what had become a dark and lonely spot overlooking the Savannah River, the Osteens repeat the actions of the very first settlers who, under Oglethorpe's direction, set up their homes and shops along the river bluff. And finally, by surrounding herself with the colors she has designed, Ann joins in the tradition of entrepreneurial Savannahians who worked hard to translate the area's local resources into useful products through which they shared the beauty and bounty of their region with the world.

Elegant Eccentricity

The Ash House
Home of the Hinsons

above: Federal style simplicity and symmetry characterizes the elegant facade of this 1817 townhouse.

right: Within the house, eccentric decorative details offset the restrained gravity of the architecture.

Eccentricity is a Southern birthright and a Savannah tradition. The city is proud to lay claim to Flannery O'Connor, a native of Savannah and one of the South's best-known chroniclers of the Gothic and grotesque aspects of human nature. The city's inhabitants have also been surprisingly tolerant of the freak-show aspect of *Midnight in the Garden of Good and Evil*, which exposed their deep vein of quirkiness to international attention. Perhaps this is because Savannahians, like most Southerners, are not embarrassed by their peculiarities. Instead, they cherish them as outward signs of their inner complexity-proof that they were, and remain, a unique people with a distinctive regional character.

In trying to explain the roots and reasons behind his own unusual style, designer Scot Hinson immediately refers to the writings of O'Connor. "Someone once asked Flannery O'Connor why Southern authors have a penchant for writing about freaks," he recounts, "and she replied that it is simply because as Southerners we are still able to recognize them." He also paraphrases fictional character Dixie Carter of television's *Designing Women*, saying, "in the South, we don't hide our freaks in the closet, we put them right in the middle of the living room." So how does this relate to style? According to Hinson, "Southerners have a tendency to introduce unexpected elements in their most formal rooms." He illustrates his point by describing the Charleston home of a friend of his mother. "She used to smoke cigars in a room filled with Ming dynasty china, fine antiques, and bird cages," he recalls. "There were at least twenty-five bird cages throughout the house and yard for her cockatoo, which still roamed free most of the time."

Although he grew up in Charleston, Hinson settled in Savannah after attending the Savannah College of Art and Design as a studio art major. He claims that he fell under

the spell of the city, an incantation made up of equal parts tradition, eccentricity, and decay. "If anyone has held on to tradition, it's Savannah," he explains. "Throw in our local characters and the falling down grandeur of the buildings, and it becomes a fascinating place." Hinson's home, one of the oldest in the city, is a perfect microcosm of the aspects he admires about Savannah. Caught mid-stream in a prolonged restoration, the house displays in several rooms and in the overgrown garden behind the decay that its owner so admires. While these unrenovated areas are off limits to visitors, hints of decay can also be found in the entertaining rooms, where the unpainted plaster ceiling reveals marble-like variations of color on its worn surface.

Tradition is evident everywhere in the house, beginning with its facade. Built in 1817 for John Ash as one of a pair of attached townhouses, the house on the northeast corner of Orleans Square displays the elegant restraint characteristic of Federal architecture. Largely unornamented brick walls and symmetrically spaced door and window openings, including a pair of white wooden dormers adorned with fan-light windows, present a pleasing regularity. Later Victorian additions have for the most part been removed with the exception of an iron balcony, which adds a delicately decorative element to the rather reserved facade.

Within, the first sight that meets the eye is a colorful mural in the entrance hall, a large-scale rendition of Tiepolo's *Banquet of Cleopatra*. This homage to Tiepolo testifies to Hinson's passion for the light, color, and composition of Italian Renaissance painting and his reverence for the classical traditions. These devotions also infuse the main entertaining rooms that open off the hall. This symmetrical suite of drawing and dining rooms is ornamented with carefully matching restored details including classically inspired ceiling medallions, mantelpieces with oval shields, and a door surround adorned with fluted pilasters. After studying houses of the same period, Hinson chose to paint the mantels and moldings in traditional shades of greenish-grey. On the waxed heart-pine floors he placed rugs of woven grass.

Despite the centuries-old tradition of using such mats in the summertime, their choice as a year-round floor covering signals a more iconoclastic approach to decorating. And indeed, the remainder of decorative decisions shaping these two rooms cross over the line from the traditional to the unexpected, revealing Hinson's persistent inclination toward the eccentric. While the sinuous curves of the grand piano and elongated legs of the Greek colonnade-style dining table reaffirm the rooms' old fashioned air of refinement, the earthy grass rugs and rustic objects including antique iron fire dogs, a folk portrait and an earthenware jar lend a less formal atmosphere. Playful elements such as 19th-century Belgian garden chandeliers converted to indoor use and bull's-eye mirrors ringed with porcupine quills offer whimsical notes that remind visitors not to take themselves-or these rooms-too seriously.

"These are a new twist on an old classic," says Hinson of the quill mirrors, which he designed, inspired both by traditional bull's-eye mirrors and 1950's sunburst medallions. While such pleasing contradictions may seem purely personal, a reflection of Hinson's own exquisite taste, the artist and designer sees them as part and parcel of a collective Southern style. "Southerners have a deep sense of formality," he explains. "We grew up with all these old things and old ways, and we cling to them by force of habit. But we also feel a need to challenge these traditions-to upset the formalities our mothers made us live with until we were sick of them."

"I am not into 'fine-fine' antiques," declares Hinson, who is an avid scavenger as well as the designer of his own line of furniture and decorative objects, which are available through his shop, Mode. "I prefer things that are scarred and scratched and rich with history. Simplicity, fresh color, and classic lines that last forever are what matter to me." In keeping with this philosophy, a pair of reupholstered flea market sofas shares the drawing room floor with 1950s bentwood and wicker armchairs, a grand piano, and a signed Gillow writing desk. The cherry red sofas provide a high voltage note against the muted, traditional paint colors Hinson chose for the room.

A tour of the rest of the house reveals a free-wheeling range of influences ranging from a modern classicist's love of art and antiques to a post-modernist's ennui, which is best summed up in a mixed-media work-on-paper entitled "Blah, blah, blah." An informal naturalist who shares Leonardo da Vinci's admiration for both the order and violence of nature, Hinson collects taxidermied birds, small animal bones, and other zoological specimens, which crop up unnervingly in the dark corners of the upstairs rooms. Other collections of odd objects displayed here and there-handleless teacups and Masonic bric-a-brac-reveal the magpie nature of an insatiable collector.

Not surprisingly, Hinson professes an aversion to house museums and private homes that are decorated impeccably to any one period. "They have a level of irreality," he complains. "People didn't really live that way." In his own home, Hinson celebrates the unruly alternative, creating eclectic, anachronistic rooms rife with odd and unexpected elements that exude a complex style as genuine and unpredictable as Southern life itself.

Taxidermized birds and brushed aluminum lamps flank a Victorian bed. The monotone grid of Hinson's painting, "Blah-blah-blah," echoes the geometries of a quilt pieced by his grandmother.

A collection of cups with no handles reveals Hinson's appreciation for the odd and unusual.

The Morris Sternberg House
Home of Neil Robinson

above: Robust mansions designed in the Romanesque Revival style proliferated in Savannah in the late 19th century.

right: This oak mantel with a variegated tile surround reflects the influence of the English Arts and Crafts movement.

Mounted upon the walls of Neil Robinson's cavernous entertaining rooms, portraits of kings and queens survey their surroundings with supercilious ease. While perhaps not as grand as the palaces these monarchs frequented in English and Continental seats of power, these new world quarters still resonate with old world sensibilities. Walls painted a deep shade of terra cotta, windows hung with yards of red and gold silk curtains, faded tapestries, 18th-century, French court furniture, and Sevres and Worcester porcelain all look as if they belong in the London townhome of a jaded scion of fallen aristocracy. And that is exactly the idea.

"It feels like Europe, like London," Robinson agrees, "which is the way our Southern minds think." He goes on to embellish his definition of what he calls the Southern mystique by saying, "People who didn't have a great deal of money after the war were often surrounded by very grand furnishings and things that were passed down from generation to generation." To make his point, he describes an acquaintance in nearby Charleston who lives in a modest bungalow surrounded by fabulous 18th-century, family heirlooms. In Robinson's case, most of his 18th-century furniture is collected, not inherited (although as an only child he did come into a cache of antiques). And his house, a brick townhouse designed in the Richardson Romanesque style in 1891 by Alfred Eichberg, hardly qualifies as a bungalow. Yet a distinct aura of fallen gentry hangs in the air of his massive double drawing room. Perhaps it is lent by the undeniable signs of decay that mark the many fine objects in the room.

"I don't mind things that are cracked and chipped and already used," says Robinson, who has compulsively collected antiques for years. In fact, Robinson seems to prefer objects that reveal their age and tell a story in the process. One of his favorite possessions is a Jacobean stool

When Neil Robinson bought this house 25 years ago, the now lavishly curtained windows were covered in cardboard and bare lightbulbs hung from the ceilings instead of chandeliers.

An 18th-century chair purchased from the estate of
Babe Paley, who upholstered it in silver leather, adds
a touch of glamour to this dining room corner.

with a disintegrating tapestry cover, which he believes may
be original. Similarly tattered pillows made from 17th-
century tapestries are purported to have been designed by
Lord Duveen for a Hudson River estate in the 1920s. Still
bright and shining, an 18th-century chair upholstered in
silver leather was purchased from the estate of Babe Paley
who, according to Robinson, "did everything in silver leaf
back in the sixties, then got tired of it." A faded tapestry
hanging near the chair looks as though it might date back
more than a century or two, but it is actually a fragment of a
set of fragile curtains, circa 1915, that Robinson purchased
from a nearby house. More antiques with fascinating
provenance include a jardiniere that came from the estate of
Vivien Leigh and a Fabergé medallion that once graced the
hat of an officer in the court of Tsar Alexander III.

These prized possessions sit on antique tables in
Robinson's double-drawing room, a room so large that a
grand piano practically disappears in one corner. Across the
front of the room, a bay of windows with mixed clear and
colored panes overlooks Jones Street when the ample red
curtains are drawn open. But these are more often closed,
shielding the interior from the hot Southern sun. A
reproduction French bureau-plat desk where Robinson
conducts his correspondence stands before the window.
Nearby, a large Famille Rose vase contains a Manet-like
arrangement of dried and silk flowers that blooms brightly
beneath a life-size portrait of an ermine-clad monarch.
"The ceilings were so tall, I bought the painting simply to
fill up wall space," says Robinson of the likeness of King
George I, which is attributed to John Shackleton and was
probably painted from life. "At the time, portraits were less
expensive than a big breakfront or secretary," he adds.
Looking around at his collection, which also includes
likenesses of Mary II, George IV, and an unknown English
noblewoman, Robinson laughingly admits with a Southern

touch of hyperbole, "For a while, I was buying all the big
paintings in England."

Glamourous and exotic objects abound in the room:
foliated wall sconces with tall candles, an intricately adorned
Chinese Chippendale mirror, an 18th century Chinese
screen, Meissen figures, and long-legged antique tables. The
dining room, lit by a crystal chandelier that reflects in a
massive pier mirror purchased from the old DeSoto Hotel, is
equally deluxe in its decor. Large Tiffany silver chargers, an
Edwardian tea service, and a pair of candelabra grace a
sideboard made in Baltimore circa 1820. A life-size likeness
of King George IV, resplendent in academic regalia,
overlooks the room. Yet despite the grandeur of these fine
accouterments, the atmosphere of the first floor entertaining
rooms is not stifling in its formality.

"I think because everything shows certain signs of age,"
Robinson surmises, "you can see that the chairs are meant
to be sat on, the rugs are meant to be walked on, and dogs
are welcome here." Perhaps it was this exquisite balance of
elegance and insouciance that inspired Manhattan socialite
Lee Radziwill to write these words after visiting with
Robinson during a Historic Savannah Foundation tour of
the city: "By comparison, hospitality doesn't seem to exist
in New York." A frequent host for honored guests of the
Foundation, Robinson has long entertained visitors from
far and near in a style that advertises not only Southern
hospitality, but also eccentricity. "I used to have a baby pig
living in my courtyard," Robinson recounts. "I'd found him
by the side of the road. When the Historic Savannah
Foundation guests would be having drinks on my back
porch, they'd see him and want their picture taken with
him. I had to give him away when he started rooting in the
wisteria."

Although the pig is gone, Robinson now shares his
domain with Stoney, a bichon whose frothy white coiffeur

On the second floor, electric light fixtures dating from the 1920's electrification of the house are still in use.

rivals that of the monarchs hanging on the walls. Most of the time, Stoney and his master occupy the small library or kitchen at the back of the house or the expansive bedroom suite on the second floor. There, the furnishings are definitely less grand, but no less genteel. The master bedroom includes a plantation-made four-poster bed of heart pine and an Edwardian reproduction of a Louis XIV settee accented with another of Lord Duveen's tapestry pillows. Artwork covers the walls including a portrait of John Jacob Astor's niece painted in Paris circa 1912 and a sepia-toned photograph of Robinson's great-grandfather in his Confederate Army uniform.

An iron light fixture dating from the early 1900s hangs from the ceiling where the paint is beginning to peel. Similar fixtures hang in the other rooms, most missing a light bulb or two. The plaster is a veined with craquelure on this floor and the furnishings are far more eclectic and less exalted than their downstairs neighbors. But Robinson doesn't worry about that. Instead, he reclines in the twilight on an old sofa in the large chamber he uses as a dressing room and gazes across his domain, drink in hand and dog recumbent at his feet. "Just look at these rooms," he exclaims, gesturing through a wide doorway to his bedroom and the sitting room beyond. "What a wonderful place to live. Aren't we fortunate?"

House of Dreams

The Francis Sorrel House
The Home of Callan Pinckney

There are three kinds of Southerners: those who never leave, those who go and stay away in a permanent state of exile, and those who travel far abroad only to return, drawn by a deep desire for the place they left behind. Callan Pinckney belongs to this last ilk. The best-selling author of Callanetics, a book and videotape describing a revolutionary approach to fitness, Callan has enjoyed worldwide success, publishing a total of nine books and eight videotapes, three of which went platinum and three gold. Before launching this phenomenal career, which brought her fame and fortune and sent her touring around the world, Callan had already circumnavigated the globe under distinctly different circumstances.

Having grown up in Savannah's Ardsley Park, a descendant of South Carolina's august Pinckney family, Callan left her hometown at the age of 21 with little more than a few hundred dollars in her pocket and a deep thirst for adventure. "I woke up one morning and said to myself, just a moment—there's a big world out there," she recalls. "I bought a rucksack and started walking around the world. I thought my walkabout would take six months, but it lasted eleven years and took me everywhere but Russia and South America." Callan's journey carried her through Europe, Africa, Asia, and beyond. She traveled by hitching rides on trucks, trains, donkeys, and anything that moved. "I lived in Nepal when there was still no electricity," she recounts, "and lost track of time for two years in Burma."

In her backpack, Callan carried a snakebite kit, a net to protect herself from insects, and a sweater, which she claims to have been her most precious possession. "I wore it in the mountains for warmth and when I slept in the luggage rack on trains, I used it as a pillow. I swore to myself that if I ever had a western style bed again, it would be a very high bed that I had to leap up on and it would have pillows, lots and lots of pillows."

In her Savannah home, a tall, deep, extremely private townhouse overlooking Madison Square, Callan has made this dream come true. The centerpiece of her bedroom is a massive four-poster canopy bed draped in yards and yards of antique French and Belgian lace and mounded high with a dozen pillows in all shapes and sizes. A French doll clad in lace hangs on the wall gazing down over the bed. "She is my guardian angel," says Callan, who clearly had one watching over her during her early travels. "I used to sleep under trucks and in alley ways and occasionally even napped in trees," she remembers, "which was stupid, because elephants used to push them over to eat the roots."

The lavish home Callan has created for herself provides a retreat from both the persistent memories of her treacherous journeys and the glamorous but grueling demands of her days as fitness phenom. In 1995, after having had enough of life in the spotlight, Callan bought a second home in Savannah to provide a getaway from her Sutton Place apartment in New York. "I thought, I'm going back to my hometown…a soft and gentle town…a place to recover the gentleness of life," she explains. "Everything in this house is here to remind me of femininity—to help me to remember that I'm not out there anymore fighting the world with my Turkish knife," she adds, referring to the weapon she used to protect herself against unwelcome advances from foreign men. "That's what all the cherubs and dolls are about."

Although she has no children, Callan has devoted an entire room to dolls. Little girls dressed in their mothers' hats and gloves are sometimes invited to participate in pretend tea parties in this room. Pink and cream colored toile covers the walls and the windows are draped with antique lace pinned with tiny porcelain fairies arrayed in frilly gowns. These elaborate draperies, as well as nearly all the other curtains and window cornices in the home, are

In keeping with the traditional Savannah floor plan, this townhouse features a side hall paralleling a pair of large and elegantly appointed entertaining rooms.

hand crafted by Callan herself. Twin beds are crowned with canopies entwined with ivy and sweetheart roses beneath which dolls dressed for christenings, weddings, and tea parties rest in frozen attitudes of make-believe. A pair of dolls made from socks belonged to Callan as a child, but most of the others, ranging from antique china baby dolls to delicate ballerinas, were collected on her international publicity tours.

In contrast with her early peregrinations, these later expeditions were well-financed affairs including expensive buying sprees at antique shops in European cities. "I bought whatever I liked," Callan declares, "as long as it was elegant, old, and refined. Coming from Savannah, you can't have new furniture," she quips. "I love antique furniture, porcelain, and old master paintings. I would crawl on my knees and go without food for an old master painting I fancied," she adds, and considering her history, this statement is likely not hyperbole. And old master paintings do, in fact, hang in the entertaining rooms of Callan's house, a Greek Revival home built for Francis Sorrel in 1856.

Ornamented with matching marble mantels carved with clustered grapes and original floral ceiling medallions from which hang crystal chandeliers, these rooms are extravagantly appointed. A portrait of a languid English noblewoman by Lely, court painter to King Charles II, hangs over the mantel and a 17th-century portrait of King Charles XI of Sweden dominates the opposing wall. Large porcelain urns commissioned by Napoleon to commemorate battles at Fleures and Rivoli sit on the mantle, flanking a gilded clock decorated with capering cherubs. Delicate French antiques with attenuated legs and intricate inlay provide several seating areas in the room's long expanse, and draperies of persimmon colored silk cascade from floor-to-ceiling windows overlooking the square below.

In the dining room, more portraits hang upon the walls including a massive life-size likeness of a dark-haired beauty whose heavy satin gown slips to reveal a pair of luminous shoulders. This portrait, painted by Irish artist Thomas Hickey, once graced the collection of a magnate whose corporate holdings included White Shoulders perfume. A smaller portrait of an Italian beauty displays decollatage to advantage as well. "I love that little one because she's wearing ermine," Callan confides.

The dining room floor is covered by a large silk Persian carpet woven with complex designs in pastel tones that echo the glazes of the Royal Copenhagen urns displayed against the pale peach walls on stands and console tables. On the dining table, Callan has arranged a whimsical centerpiece of porcelain nymphs and cherubs inspired by a childhood memory of visits to an Ardsley Park neighbor who displayed a similar centerpiece. "I always dreamed of owning one myself," says Callan, who later found the set at an antique store and sent it home at once.

Although she occasionally invites special groups to tour her home, Callan admits that she never entertains. "I have quite a collection of silver, but no china to go with it because all the old place settings I love have lead in them," she explains. "I'd have to serve dinner on paper plates, and that would be scandalous!" Instead, she prefers to keep her large house to herself. "I've created a setting for myself," says Callan, who decorated the house entirely without the guidance of interior designers. With its fine art and rare antiques, this setting conjures up the old world elegance of the European capitals Callan toured as a celebrity as well as the lavish Southern style her Pinckney forebears enjoyed in nearby Charleston in centuries past. But the house's distinct decor, bordering on the eccentric and extreme, also expresses a far more personal, less tangible ideal-a nomadic Southerner's dreams of home.

This second-floor bedroom, draped with yards of antique European lace, creates an ultra-feminine, oh-so-Southern retreat from the world.

An Enduring Hospitality

The Isaiah Davenport House
A House Museum of Historic Savannah
Foundation

above: Designed in the late Georgian/early Federal styles, this stately house barely escaped demolition in the 1950s when it was nearly razed to make room for a parking lot.

right: A pair of Ionic columns ornament the center hall which also features a dramatic serpentine stairway.

Designed both as a symbol of the success and a showpiece for the talent of an enterprising young builder, nearly destroyed to make room for a funeral parlor parking lot, and rescued and restored as one of the city's beloved house museums, the Isaiah Davenport House is one of the most moving relics of Savannah's architectural history. Constructed of durable brick and brownstone, standing high upon a raised basement, and approached by a curved double stairway, it testifies to both the elegant tastes and ambitious aspirations of early-19th-century Savannahians.

Like most citizens in his day, Isaiah Davenport was an outsider attracted to the city by the possibility of attaining wealth and position in its rapidly expanding economy. He moved to Savannah in 1807 from Rhode Island in his early 20s, having completed an apprenticeship as a house-builder in New Bedford, Massachusetts. Well versed in the Georgian and Federal principles of design, which had enjoyed widespread popularity in more established American centers of wealth, Davenport quickly secured commissions in Savannah's early-19th-century building boom. With the city still recovering from a devastating fire in 1796 and growing fast in the wake of the invention of the cotton gin and subsequent expansion of the cotton trade, Davenport quickly fulfilled his aspirations for success.

The young builder married Sarah Rosamond Clark from Beaufort, South Carolina in 1809 and purchased a corner lot overlooking Columbia Square three years later. But Davenport was so busy building houses for his growing clientele that he could not design his own house until 1820. By then, he had not only attained recognition and reward as a house-builder, but was also a rising public servant whose positions included fire master and constable and city alderman. The house he finally built served not only as a home for Davenport's growing family, but also as the headquarters for his business, with a small office on the parlor

In an office on the parlor floor, Isaiah Davenport conducted his architectural trade during the seven years he occupied this house before his death.

floor. It was also a center for social activities, with sumptuous entertaining rooms that demonstrated the high position the Davenports had so quickly gained in Savannah society.

Even though William Jay had already introduced the newer English Regency style to Savannah by the time Davenport designed his home, the house-builder remained faithful to the traditional styles in which he had been trained. The brick and brownstone house he built has a Georgian stateliness, flanked on two sides by four tall chimneys and balanced around a center hall. The most notable features of the simple exterior are its raised basement, which may have set the standard for future Savannah dwellings, and the graceful double stairway ornamented with delicate wrought-iron railings. While handsome and elegant, the restrained facade does little to prepare the visitor for the lavishly detailed interior rooms, which clearly demonstrate Davenport's knowledge of classical motifs and his facility with decorative detail.

The "proportion of public to private space on [the] main floor and elaborateness of plaster decoration . . . suggests [Davenport's] desire to impress and entertain," notes Richard Ruehrwein in his brief history of the house.[1] Certainly, it is impossible to enter the Davenport House without at once recognizing that it was designed by a master builder. Although the center hall is narrow, it frames a dramatic view through a pair of free-standing Ionic columns of an unsupported serpentine stairway that spirals up three flights. Halfway up the first landing, a tall arched window welcomes in the light and air. On the heart-pine floor, a heavily shellacked canvas painted to resemble elaborate marble parquet gleams with reflected light.

To the right of this hall lies the house's most elaborate room, a large rectangular drawing room. Two delicately proportioned elliptical arches supported by Ionic columns span the full width of the room on two sides. One arch frames the entrance to the morning room and the other one rises above a pair of windows overlooking Columbia Square. Fancy plaster cornice moldings in anthemia and rosette patterns encircle the ceiling, adding even more layers of intricate detail to the highly decorated room. In the center of one wall is an Italian marble mantle, which, though original to the house, was missing for several decades. The story behind the mantel's peregrinations reveals the tragedies that shaped the history of the house soon after it was completed.

Isaiah Davenport died of yellow fever only seven years after completing his elegant home. With six children under the age of 13 and a seventh child on the way, his widow was forced to find a way to make ends meet. An advertisement that appeared in the Savannah newspaper not long after Isaiah's death is a poignant reminder of the efforts she made to keep her household intact. "Mrs. Davenport has determined not to rent the house belonging to the estate of Isaiah Davenport and proposes to open a private Boarding House on the 5th of November," the 1827 notice read. "From the situation and general convenience of the House, and her attention to the accommodation and comfort of those who may favor the undertaking, she hopes to receive a share of the public patronage and asks the interest of her friends in effecting the object."[2]

Sadly, Sarah's efforts did not raise enough income to cover mounting taxes, and ultimately she was forced to sell the house and find a more modest one in which to raise her family. As Savannah's fortunes rose and fell over the next century, the house passed through several owners until, in the 1930s, it was reduced to the state of a shabby tenement in a neighborhood that was little more than a slum. The elegant rooms had been subdivided into small apartments lit by dangling, naked light bulbs and stripped of any decorative elements that could be sold, including mantels and crystal chandeliers. With its interior columns painted black and floral paper covering the walls, the decrepit house bore little semblance to its original grandeur. Old photographs show the facade, robbed of its wooden shutters, looking blank and bare.

While the house was in this sad and vulnerable state, Katherine Summerlin, step-daughter of Mr. Goette of the nearby Goette Funeral Home, took title to the property and prepared to raze it to make room for a parking lot. When she discovered this plan, Mrs. Anna Hunter, a painter and journalist, quickly mobilized a number of friends who shared her passion for preserving Savannah's architectural jewels. Together these seven ladies, also including Mrs. Rueben Clark, Miss Jane Adair Wright, Miss Lucy B. McIntire, Mrs. Louis Roos, Mrs. William Dillard, and Mrs. C.C. Roebling, raised the money needed to purchase the property and convinced Katherine Summerlin to sell it to their new organization, Historic Savannah Foundation, in 1955. This organization supervised the restoration of the Davenport House, raising additional funds and seeking

Tapering Ionic columns support matching elliptical arches on either end of the rectangular drawing room, demonstrating Davenport's facility with complicated classical decoration to his guests and potential clients.

contributions of period furniture that complemented the house's early 19th century design. Among these gifts was a mantelpiece donated in 1998-the original Italian marble mantel that Davenport had chosen to grace his drawing room more than a century before.

Today, visitors can tour the rooms that have been been carefully furnished with Chippendale, and Sheraton pieces that bear close resemblance to those described in an inventory made of the Davenports' property a year after Isaiah's death. Marble mantels again adorn the rooms, as well as crystal chandeliers and curtains made of silk. Sarah Davenport's family album, featuring curled locks of various family members' hair, sits once more in the master bedroom. And old toys and cradles crowd the attic rooms where the Davenports' six sons once played and slept. Although a crowd of strangers passes through these rooms all day-tourists seeking insights into the lives and styles of old Savannahians-it seems quite likely that familiar spirits may frequent them at night, ghosts of the people who lived too briefly in this house returning to enjoy its enduring hospitality.

High Victorian Romanticism

The Baldwin House
Home of Alvin Neely

Savannah is full of surprises, and the prevalence of massive brick and terra cotta mansions in the Queen Anne and Richardsonian Romanesque styles is one of them. Thoughts of Savannah, or of any major center of the antebellum South, generally tend toward images of pale and stately facades ornamented in the Greek or other Classical Revival styles. "Because there was so little building in the South at the time, High Victorian architecture never swept the region as it did the rest of the country," wrote noted architectural historian, Kenneth Severens. "The South was largely spared the intrusion of Victorian irregularity and eccentricity."[1] Fortunately, Savannah was an exception to the rule and structures like the Baldwin House stand as eloquent defenders of the oft-maligned high Victorian romantic styles.

This is not to say that many Savannahians were not at first startled by the introduction of these fanciful structures amid their sleepy wards. Even present-day architectural historians consider them dramatic, including former Oxford professor James Cox who described these buildings as "rambunctious essays in red or yellow brick exploiting novel shapes and highly romantic skylines[.]"[2] But in the late 19th century, Savannah's leading businessmen sought out architects to create public and private buildings in the most stylish contemporary modes in an effort to reclaim the city's pre-war status as a thriving center of culture and commerce. Having won a national competition to design Savannah's new Cotton Exchange, William Gibbons Preston came to the city in 1886. A prominent architect from Boston, Preston was a Harvard graduate who, like his better-known contemporary Henry Hobson Richardson, completed his studies at the Ecole des Beaux Arts in Paris.

The Baldwin House combines the hallmarks of Richardsonian Romanesque and Queen Anne architecture with its massive Roman arches, textured surfaces of pressed brick interspersed with cast terracotta and waffle pattern detail, and fanciful fenestration.

This cavernous entrance hall, which opens into a series of entertaining rooms, easily accommodated the large gatherings of people who attended the Baldwin family's legendary parties.

George Baldwin, an influential member of the Cotton Exchange board at the time, was so impressed by Preston's vision and style that he hired him to design his own residence and widely championed the architect, who secured four more major institutional commissions within five years. Both Baldwin and Preston rode the wave of prosperity that was transforming Savannah into a bold center of the New South in the post-war decades-and left the lasting mark of their enthusiasm for innovation upon the city's fabric.

The Queen Anne style, as executed by Preston and other contemporaries, defied the conventional form of Savannah houses, typically long structures with a linear progression of rectangular rooms. In shape, the home Preston designed for Baldwin recalls the Gothic manor hall instead with a large central stair hall forming its heart. This cavernous chamber is flanked by an asymmetrical arrangement of rooms in an array of shapes: circle, octagon, and rectangle. Stained glass windows punctuate the interior's dark oak paneling, and once-bright murals and decorative borders painted upon the ceilings and walls add yet another level of color and detail.

Free-wheeling influences intertwine to create an exuberant eclecticism: a stylized floral motif in the octagonal library evokes Moorish design; the heavily beamed ceiling of the stair hall pays homage to English precedents; and columns and pilasters with Corinthian capitals refer to both ancient Greece and the more recent, regional Greek Revival style. On the exterior, soaring Romanesque arches with terra cotta capitals define a portico. A turret capped with a pepper-pot dome and a stepped gable in the Dutch manner create an asymmetrical, whimsical roofline. In a city where stylistic eclecticism and architectural inventiveness had long enjoyed popularity, the Baldwin House managed to raise the aesthetic bar even higher.

It is only fitting that the man who commissioned it was a maverick entrepreneur of the New South—an innovator who ushered in new technologies that transformed the region he called home. George Baldwin started his career at his father's firm, Baldwin & Company, an august establishment dealing in traditional Savannah commodities of cotton, naval supplies, and fertilizer. But he soon branched out into developing technologies. While maintaining a seat on the Savannah Cotton Exchange, Baldwin became a mogul in electric railway and lighting plants. Founder and President of the Savannah Electric Company, he also presided over the Gainesville Midland Railway, a steam railroad running out of Gainesville, and the electric railway and lighting companies of Jacksonville, Tampa, Key West, and Pensacola, Florida. A former engineering student at the Massachusetts Institute of Technology, Baldwin also designed the electric trolley system for Savannah and several other southern cities.

With the help of his wife Lucy, Baldwin also succeeded in breaking new ground in the arena of hospitality in Savannah, despite the city's long-standing reputation for lavish parties. With its flowing arrangement of entertaining rooms, wrap-around porch, and ample guest rooms, the couple's house was ideally suited for large gatherings. Baldwin's 1927 obituary describes his house as "the center of social and cultural life" in Savannah. Current resident Alvin Neely continues this tradition, giving parties in support of Historic Savannah Foundation and other local charities, and hosting reunions of Baldwin family descendants.

Neely, who has become the house's unofficial curator, describes two legendary entertainments that took place in the house: the Baldwin's house-warming party and their daughter Dorothea's debut. Peter Sherry, New York City's most fashionable caterer, was employed to oversee the first of these. "Everything came down by steamship," says Neely:

"the food, the wine, the orchestra, even the head waiter." Clearly impressed, one of the guests described it in a letter as "the grandest party ever." For the second party, a temporary room was built in the backyard for the party's 500 guests. An old black-and-white photo of the structure shows elaborate faux-architectural detail and floral decorations.

Neely's collection of old photographs traces the many changes the Baldwin's house underwent following the family's departure after thirty years of residence. The subsequent inhabitants tried to tone down the house's bold décor, painting much of the dark paneling white and adding new friezes in Classical Revival styles over the glazed, textured, and stenciled walls. Delicately detailed parquet was installed over the heart-pine flooring. A wall was added between the reception room and library, breaking up the fluid progression of spaces, and original built-in furniture features including a china cabinet and a sewing table were removed.

During his near thirty years of residence, Neely has done his best to undo these modifications to the house's original robust design and to reestablish its Queen Anne flavor. With the help of students from the Savannah College of Art and Design, he has restored many of the original wall colors and removed layers of plaster cloth that obscured the original Arts and Crafts detailing on the walls and ceilings. One of the most dramatic moments during this ongoing project occurred when the plaster cloth fell off the ceiling in Neely's bedroom as he slept. His four-poster bed, a Charleston-made antique, saved his life by breaking the fall of the fifteen-foot clump.

In an effort to reproduce the warm patina of the house's original surfaces, Neely simply painted a coat of shellac over the bedroom's newly revealed plaster. He hired artists to design a floral motif border inspired by the flowering vines of Confederate jasmine for the room's

perimeter and asked a friend's mother to crochet the bed's old-fashioned canopy cover. The large Oriental rug on the bedroom floor-so worn it bears only the faintest trace of pattern-echoes the faded amber tones of the ceiling. Stacked with piles of papers and books, this bed/sitting room serves as an informal office for Neely, a retired English teacher and avid reader.

The rooms below, while frequently used for their original purpose of entertaining, also serve Neely's solitary lifestyle well. "I spend most of my time in the library or on the porch," he confesses. Although it was designed for a very different set of residents-a family with a full retinue of servants and pressing social responsibilities-the house suits its current inhabitant well. And his array of inherited furnishings, designed in a range of Victorian and Edwardian tastes, perfectly complements the house's style. Even Neely's extensive collection of wrought-metal bridge lamps, with their quirky silhouettes, seems right at home.

"This is a house with a good feeling about it," Neely says. "It has brought happiness to the people who lived here . . . and it has influenced my life every day that I've lived in it." Describing it as his "one-and-only house," Neely dedicates himself to its care just as the poets he loves to read-Chaucer, Conrad Aiken, and W.H. Auden-committed themselves to their craft. Perfecting and polishing one small aspect at a time, removing an inappropriate element here and adding a perfect embellishment there, he celebrates the complex life and art of this particular place.

This receiving room provided guests a resting place while servants conveyed their calling cards to members of the Baldwin Family.

The spacious porch is comfortably furnished with a wicker day bed, rocking chairs, and occasional tables that once graced the porch of Alvin Neely's childhood home in nearby Waynesboro, Georgia.

The Gift of Place

Wormsloe
Home of Mr. and Mrs. Craig Barrow, III

The history of Wormsloe can be described as a centuries-long sequence of gifts—gifts given lightly with no thought of repayment and gifts given ponderously with every intention of engendering a deep sense of stewardship within the recipient. The first recorded gift, which shaped the life of seven subsequent generations of a Georgia family, was of the second sort. Soon after Georgia was founded, its trustees granted land along a tidewater river to Noble Jones who, along with his family, was among the first colonists to arrive. In return for this gift, Jones was commanded to build a fort overlooking the river to protect the fledgling colony from Indians and Spaniards from Florida. Later, Jones received more acreage in exchange for his promise to cultivate the land. Even the property's name, Wormsloe, was given with the intent of inspiring a result: the cultivation of mulberry trees and silk worms. But the virgin land, which proved unsuitable for silk production, resisted this last command. Little large-scale cultivation ever occurred on Wormsloe's 800 acres, which today retains the majestic and mysterious quality of a primeval forest dense, with towering hardwood trees and an abundance of wildlife.

"When I wander through the woods, I think about the many different generations of people who have walked this place: the Indians, the colonists, the Revolutionary soldiers, the slaves, the Confederate and Union troops," says Craig Barrow, III, eighth-generation descendant of Noble Jones and present-day resident at Wormsloe. "I don't believe you can go anywhere else around here and know that you are experiencing the exact same landscape that so many other people have experienced over the centuries."

Craig and his wife, Diana, have a powerful feeling of stewardship for Wormsloe. From an early age, he was included in discussions with his father, Craig Barrow, Jr., and grandmother, Elfrida DeRenne Barrow, regarding the

Although its tabby foundations date from 1828, this house was dramatically remodeled in the late 19th century in the Victorian style and refashioned again in the 1930s in the graceful Classical Revival mode.

In keeping with traditional plantation architecture, the wide center hall features doors at either end, which, when open, provide cooling breezes and bright light.

preservation of the property. "My grandmother wanted to preserve Wormsloe in its natural state," Craig explains, a desire which resulted in a gift of 750 acres of the property to the State of Georgia in 1973, launching the Georgia Heritage Trust program.

Two-hundred-and-forty years after the riverside property had been given to Noble Jones so that he might, from his fort, protect the new colony from encroaching marauders, Jones's descendants gave it back to the governing powers with the same intention: to protect the land from encroachment. But this time, the interlopers in question were not Indians or Spaniards, but real estate developers who had purchased and subdivided nearly all the other original land grants, plantations, and undeveloped territory in the area. "Today,…Wormsloe is one of very few early coastal Georgia estates to survive in the era of subdivision and industrial parks[,]" wrote a visiting journalist in 1967.[1] "[I]t is the only one to remain in the family of the original owner. It is Georgia's most dramatic link to its founding."

Visitors are welcome to tour this historic site, which includes the ruins of Noble Jones's fort, a museum, and extensive woodland paths. The dramatic quality of the property is immediately evident to those who arrive at its entrance off the two-lane road that winds through the rapidly developing countryside. A massive arch grown dark with age and inscribed "Wormsloe 1733–1913" marks the approach. It is flanked by giant oak trees with sprawling branches festooned in Spanish moss. Beyond the gate, two lines of oaks stretch into the distance, their graceful bows interlacing overhead to form a seemingly endless passageway to the horizon.

This awe inspiring avenue was another gift of sorts, planted in 1891 by Wormsloe's fifth owner, Wymberley Jones DeRenne, to celebrate the birth of his son. Given to

One of a pair of double parlors, this room is decorated with inherited objects including bronze candlesticks that belonged to Elfrida DeRenne Barrow and new furnishings that complement the traditional style of the house.

A library built by Wymberley Jones DeRenne in 1907 combines a Greek Revival exterior with a Gothic style interior to create an imposing effect.

the grand gesture, DeRenne erected the entrance gate to commemorate this son's 21st birthday, as well as the Greek Revival library that stands behind the family home. This temple-like structure, though small in scale, is imposing in effect both without, with its marble stairs and towering Corinthian columns, and within, where a massive fireplace complete with gargoyles looms over the large book-lined room. A more feminine air was given to the property by Wymberley's wife, Augusta, who laid out a series of formal gardens behind the house as well as expansive plantings of camellias and azaleas. The semi-enclosed rooms, with their worn brick walls and still reflecting pool, and the meandering azalea trails, overgrown with brightly blazing bushes and strewn with marble statuary, have the still and dreamy air of Sleeping Beauty's garden.

The house has undergone several remodelings since its original foundation of tabby was laid in 1828. For nearly seventy years, a simple frame house stood on this foundation. Although a modest home not designed for year-long residence, it featured elaborate marble mantelpieces, which remain today in the double parlors. One adorned with cariatyds, the other with female figures clad in classical draperies, both mantels bear the marks of mutilation suffered at the hands of Union troops who were stationed at the property during Sherman's occupation of Savannah. This house was remodeled and expanded in the 1890s, assuming the unwieldy grandeur of a Victorian showplace, and reconfigured again in the 1930s to attain its present appearance. Sixteen rooms were removed, mostly servants' quarters, and a graceful portico added. The resulting house invokes the simple elegance of antebellum plantation architecture with tall shuttered windows, stately double stairs, and white columns ornamenting the facade.

When they moved in thirteen years ago, Craig and Diana Barrow faced the challenge of furnishing the house

TO
NOBLE JONES
OWNER OF WORMSLOE
FROM
1733 TO 1775

WORMSLOE

Planted more than 100 years ago, this majestic oak allée now welcomes not only Noble Jones's descendants but also members of the public who come to savor its timeless beauty.

in a style that both respected its past and created a comfortable environment for raising a family. "We had to decide—do we want to live in a museum or a house?" recalls Craig. The final result seems to balance the two alternatives. A quiet hospitality pervades the rooms, which appear refined without the least air of pretension. Indeed, humility and gratitude seems to be the over-riding attitudes of the present-day inhabitants towards their home. In keeping with family tradition, the Barrows continue to protect the property fiercely (funds from a family foundation were recently deployed to purchase a nearby island threatened with subdivision) and to multiply its gifts. Family contributions include the restoration of the Victorian superintendent's cottage standing beneath the shadow of the entrance gate and the replenishment of the property's deer population, initiated thirty years ago when Craig gave his father eleven deer to commemorate his 70th birthday.

As the sun sinks below the horizon, its last rays penetrate the canopy of Spanish moss that hangs from Wormsloe's oaks to illuminate the patinaed surface of a bronze deer standing in the garden. A 25th-anniversary gift to Diana, this statue will probably remain on the property for decades, if not centuries, to come as subsequent generations of this family assume their stewardship of Wormsloe. "We are so lucky to live here," Diana exclaims. "This is so much more than just a house," Craig adds, "it is a place. Wormsloe is bigger than we are."

Bibliography

Berendt, John. *Midnight in the Garden of Good and Evil*. New York: Random House, 1994.

Cox, James D. and N. Jane Iseley. *Savannah: Tour of Homes & Gardens*. Savannah: Christ Church and Historic Savannah Foundation, 1996.

Lane, Mills B. *Savannah Revisited: History and Architecture.* Savannah: The Beehive Press, 1969.

Martin, Van Jones and William Robert Mitchell, Jr. *Landmark Houses of Georgia, 1733-1983.* Savannah, GA: Golden Coast Publishing Company, 1983.

O'Connor, Flannery. Edited by Sally and Robert Fitzgerald. *Mystery and Manners: Occasional Prose.* New York: Farrar, Straus and Giroux, Inc., 1961.

Talbott, Page. *Classical Savannah.* Savannah: Telfair Museum of Art, 1995.

Toledano, Roulhac. *The National Trust Guide to Savannah, Architectural and Cultural Treasures.* Washington, DC: National Trust for Historic Preservation in cooperation with John Wiley & Son, Inc., 1997.

Notes

Introduction

1. Robert Somers, *The Southern States since the War* (London and New York: Macmillan and Co., 1871), Chapter XII.
2. John Berendt, foreword to Roulhac Toledano, *The National Trust Guide to Savannah, Architectural and Cultural Treasures* (Washington, DC: National Trust for Historic Preservation in cooperation with John Wiley & Son, Inc., 1997), p. xvii.
3. Robert Mackay, *The Letters of Robert Mackay to his Wife: Written from ports in America and England, 1795-1816* (Athens: The University of Georgia Press under the auspices of The Georgia Society of the Colonial Dames, 1949), p. 92.
4. Mills B. Lane, *Savannah Revisited: History and Architecture* (Savannah: The Beehive Press, 1969), p. 41.
5. A report by John Ettwein, who was on a business tour of Savannah in the interest of the Moravian Brethren, April 4–5, 1762 (John Ettwein Papers, 1762-65, Georgia Historical Society, Savannah).
6. Eli Whitney, in a letter dated 1793, quoted in Lane, p. 55.
7. Lane, p. 57.
8. John Pope, *John Pope: His Tour* (Richmond: John Dixon, 1792; reprint: New York: C. L. Woodward, 1888).
9. Charles S. H. Hardee, *Reminiscences and Recollections of Old Savannah* (Savannah, GA: Privately Printed, 1928), p. 61.
10. William Jay, letter to the editor, *The Daily Georgian*, Vol. II, No. 43, (January 22, 1820), p. 3, cols. 1-2.
11. James D. Cox and N. Jane Iseley, *Savannah: Tour of Homes & Gardens* (Savannah, GA: Christ Church and Historic Savannah Foundation, 1996), p. 9.
12. Fredrika Bremer, *Homes of the New World, Impressions of America*, Vol. I (New York: Harper & Brothers, Publishers, 1854), p. 340.
13. William Thackeray, *A Collection of Letters of Thackeray* (New York: Charles Scribner's Sons, 1887), p. 169.

14. Toledano, p. 38.
15. W.D. Howells, "Savannah Twice Visited," *Harper's Magazine*, No. 825 (February 1919), p. 323.
16. Toledano, pp. xvii–xviii.
17. Toledano, 1997, p. 5.
18. Berendt, "Mercer House Revisited," *Architectural Digest*, Vol. 52, No. 5 (May 1995), p. 56.
19. Ibid, p. 60.
20. Flannery O'Connor , *Mystery and Manners: Occasional Prose,* selected and edited by Sally and Robert Fitzgerald, (New York: Farrar, Straus and Giroux, Inc.: 1961), p. 35.
21. Ibid, p. 29.
22. Sara Hathaway, quoted in Lane, pp. 46-47.
23. W.D. Howells, p. 324.
24. Mrs. David Hillhouse, an 1818 visitor from interior Georgia, quoted in Lane, p. 62.
25. Julien Green, grandson of Charles Green, quoted in Van Jones Martin and William Robert Mitchell, Jr., *Landmark Houses of Georgia, 1733-1983* (Savannah, GA: Golden Coast Publishing Company, 1983), p. 100.
26. Timothy Harley, quoted in Arnold Berke, "The Ideal City," *Preservation*, vol. 50, #4 (July/Aug. 1998), p. 110.

The Houses

The Champion Harper Fowlkes House
1. Albert Sidney Britt, Jr., *The Champion, Harper-Fowlkes House*, (Headquarters, Society of the Cincinnati in the State of Georgia, Savannah: 1982; revised 1988), pp. 7–8.

The Thomas Levy House
1. Toledano, p. 155.

The Owens Thomas House
1. Page Talbott, *Classical Savannah* (Savannah: Telfair Museum of Art, 1995), p. 50.
2. James Silk Buckingham, *The Slave States of America* (London: Fisher, Son & Co., 1842), pp. 119–120; quoted in Talbott, 1995, p. 50.
3. James A.D. Cox, *Savannah Tour of Homes & Gardens* (Savannah: Christ Church & Historic Savannah Foundation, 1996), p. 8.
4. Talbott, p. 57

Lebanon Plantation
1. Medora Field Perkerson, *White Columns in Georgia* (Bonanza Books, 1952), pp. 90–93.

The Trosdal House
1. Toledano, p. 195.

Conrad Aiken's Childhood Home
1. Homes with Style, The Style Channel, 1999

The Isaiah Davenport House
1. Richard Ruehrwein, *The Davenport House* (Savannah, GA: Historic Savannah Foundation, 1995).
2. Ibid.

The Baldwin House
1. Kenneth Severens, *Southern Architecture, 350 Years of Distinctive Buildings*, 1981.
2. James Cox, *Savannah Tour of Homes and Gardens* (Christ Church and Historic Savannah Foundation, 1996).

Wormsloe
1. Lee Giffen, "Living with Antiques: Wormsloe, The Home of Mrs. Craig Barrow," *Antiques* (March 1967), pp. 370–373.

Index

Acknowledgements

There is always one person without whose help a book could not be written. In this case there are far too many even to begin to thank, but I shall make a heart-felt attempt to do so. The first of these is Celia Dunn, of Celia W. Dunn Realty Company, who has been my constant advisor, frequent hostess, and invaluable consultant through the researching and writing of this book. She literally opened the doors of Savannah for me, and I am forever in her debt. Equally essential to the creation of this book are John and Ginger Duncan, proprietors of V & J Duncan Antique Prints, Maps and Books. Without John's careful fact checking and assistance in tracking down rare primary sources, this book would not exist in its final form. Without John's and Ginger's hospitality, friendship, and encouragement, I would have had far less pleasure completing my research and writing. Many thanks are also extended to Steven Brooke, for taking such amazing photographs, and to David Morton and Damon Ferrante, for their editorial guidance.

Thanks are due to all the Savannahians who so graciously allowed a stranger from Charleston into their homes. I am always amazed by and deeply grateful for the sense of pride and joy Southerners take in sharing their homes with visitors from afar. This generosity bears fruit in the preceding pages, in which readers are offered privileged glimpses into the very private realms of Southern living.

Thank you to all those kind individuals whose houses were visited, but not selected for inclusion in the book; I wish I could include every single one, as each is a perfect expression of Savannah style. I also wish to extend my gratitude to those homeowners whose houses are included in the book–thank you for all your patience and cooperation.

A few more people require special thanks. These include Ed and Caroline Hill, for providing a place to stay as well as delightful company during my visits to Savannah; Mark McDonald of Historic Savannah Foundation and Steve Bisson of the Savannah Morning News for loaning me photographs; the staff of the Georgia Historical Society; and the President and staff of the Savannah College of Art and Design. I could not have found so many beautiful and interesting homes in Savannah without the help of Scot Hinson, Sim Harvey, Phillip Hunter, Elizabeth Demos, Paul Garguilo, Chris Johnson, Wanda Brooks, and many others. Thank you! Thanks also are due to Carl S. Weeks, author of *Savannah in the Time of Peter Tondee: The Road to Revolution in Colonial Georgia*; Paul M. Pressly, author of the article entitled "The Northern Roots of Savannah's Antebellum Elite, 1780s–1850s"; and Mills B. Lane, author of *Savannah Revisited: History and Architecture*. I benefited tremendously from their research and insights.